The Island Cookbook

Includes

RHODE ISLAND, Block Island, Newport, Jamestown, Prudence, MARTHA'S VINEYARD, and last but not least NANTUCKET

by Barbara Sherman Stetson

Illustrations by Marion King

MARION E. KING

This cookbook is a collection of recipes which are not necessarily original recipes.

Author: Barbara Sherman Stetson　　　　Illustrator: Marion King

Published by:　　Barbara Sherman Stetson
　　　　　　　　P.O. Box 822
　　　　　　　　North Scituate, Rhode Island 02857

Edited, Designed and Manufactured in the United States of America by:
Favorite Recipes® Press, an imprint of

RP™

P.O. Box 305142
Nashville, Tennessee 37230
1-800-358-0560

©1993 Stetson, Barbara Sherman

Stetson, Barbara Sherman.
　The Island Cookbook / Barbara Sherman Stetson.
　　p. cm.
　　Includes index.
　　ISBN 0-87197-370-7
　　1. Cookery—Massachusetts. 2. Cookery—Rhode Island.
　3. Massachusetts—History. 4. Rhode Island—History.　I. Title.
　TX715.S844　1993
　641.59744—dc20

93-3350
CIP

First Printing: 1993
Second Printing: 1994
Third Printing: 1995
Fourth Printing: 1999
Fifth Printing: 2001

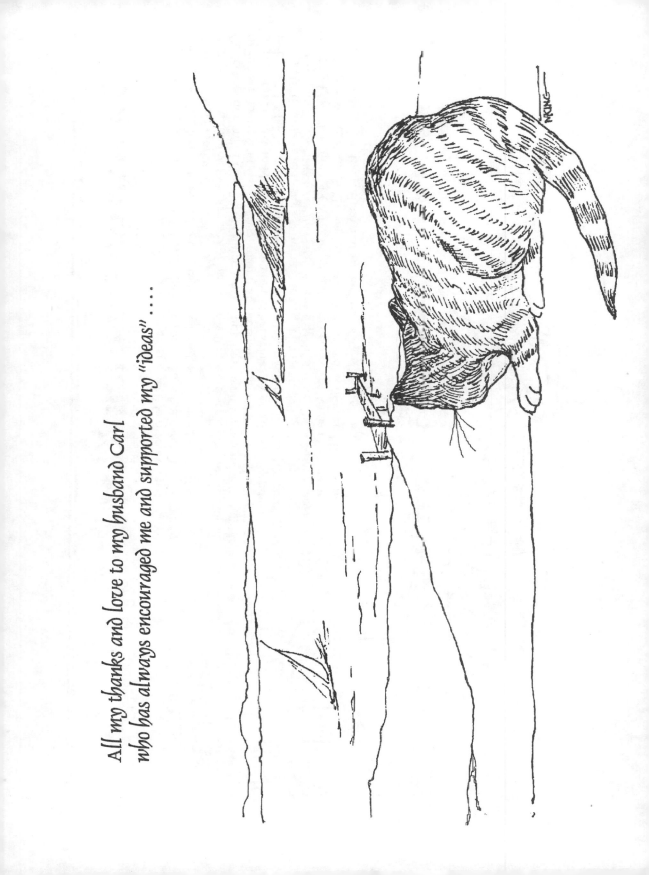

All my thanks and love to my husband Carl
who has always encouraged me and supported my "ideas" ….

The Artist—Marion King

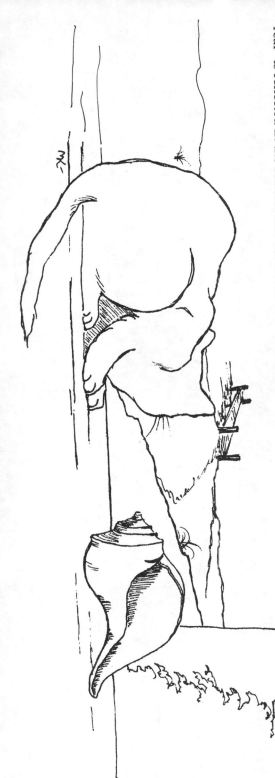

An artist of many talents, Marion King Wieselquist is well known in Rhode Island art circles. Her present career started after the birth of her son Erik. Born into a native Rhode Island family, she carries on the tradition of three generations of the noted King family.

Her outstanding wood carvings of birds and wildlife are second to none in the area. Collectors not only in the New England Area, but those who are fortunate enough to have been to the Cleveland Museum of Natural History and the American Museum of Natural History in New York have viewed her works. A creative and original individual, Marion works in many media including painting, illustrating, quilting and other textile arts—as she says "anything to avoid housework."

As an illustrator, she has "Receipts and Anecdotes of Scituate," a 369-page cookbook, by the Heritage Club and "A Cookbook of Swedish Memories" by Vivian Stenstrom, to her credit in the cookbook field. Her love of cooking, the outdoors and things that "are real" is reflected in the realism and subtle humor in her works.

Table of Contents

Preface

This is not really a cookbook but a saga of what my friends and family have listened to for over 40 years... "when I write my cookbook." *The Island Cookbook* is a reflection of past and present recipes not only from my forefathers but also from family, friends, teachers, tourist finds, and locals. Background material for this publication was derived from many sources, primarily from old receipt books, diaries, archives of many historical societies in the Islands, interviews with so many, and a review of literature available in private and public collections. To quote my husband who really put up with a lot—I don't mean the experiments, but the piles of recipes, cookbooks, clippings, old envelopes and notes from friends—he "married me because I was a good cook, not because I was a housekeeper."

Many recipes are very similar throughout the islands, so I have adapted and presented a basic recipe in many cases. Care has been taken by me and my "executive chef" Carl Herman (hubbie) Stetson of "Herman's Hideaway" to simplify, when possible,

recipes in "old time receipt form" and to test as many recipes as possible. No, we didn't gain a hundred pounds, but neither did we lose any. Oh, by the way, "Herman's Hideaway" is the name of our "at home restaurant" that is better than any we've ever been to.

Although many of the recipes have had fat, salt and sugar reduced from the originals, this is not an indication that they can be substituted in "special diets." Please consult your dietitian, nutritionist or physician if you have any questions concerning recipes for your special use.

First Law of Kitchen Confusion: In a family recipe you discover in an old book, the most vital measurement will be illegible. How true it is! Starting with my grandmother's receipts and those sent by her friends, I felt I needed a translation course for hieroglyphics. In journals in very early receipts, a list of ingredients were given, never in order of use, without time, temperature, or directions. You will really appreciate how I have changed these recipes in appearance, but I hope not taste. Many people I interviewed did not have their recipes written or in level measurements (a little of this and a little of that,) so I apologize to those I may not have interpreted exactly "like your old family recipes." As editor and

author, I took the liberty of doing the "best I could." My many thanks to all who shared with me, including old friends, new friends and those whom we met who shared their recipes and cooking hints, but who didn't introduce themselves—they have made this book both interesting and challenging. It's not just a cookbook, but a way I have interacted with people throughout my life. It certainly has been a most enjoyable project for us, meeting all of you.

My husband, Carl, who, by the way, is an excellent cook, did much of the testing of the recipes. Our friends, neighbors and associates were the "tasters." As Carl's fraternity brother of 50 years said, "I guess the cookbook will be good. I've survived 25 years of your testing." He recently left a telephone message in response to our answering machine message that we were conducting testing for the book: "When are you going to stop researching and finish the damn cookbook?" Well, Walter, Nancy and "the rest"...here it is!

Barbara Sherman Stetson
February 1993

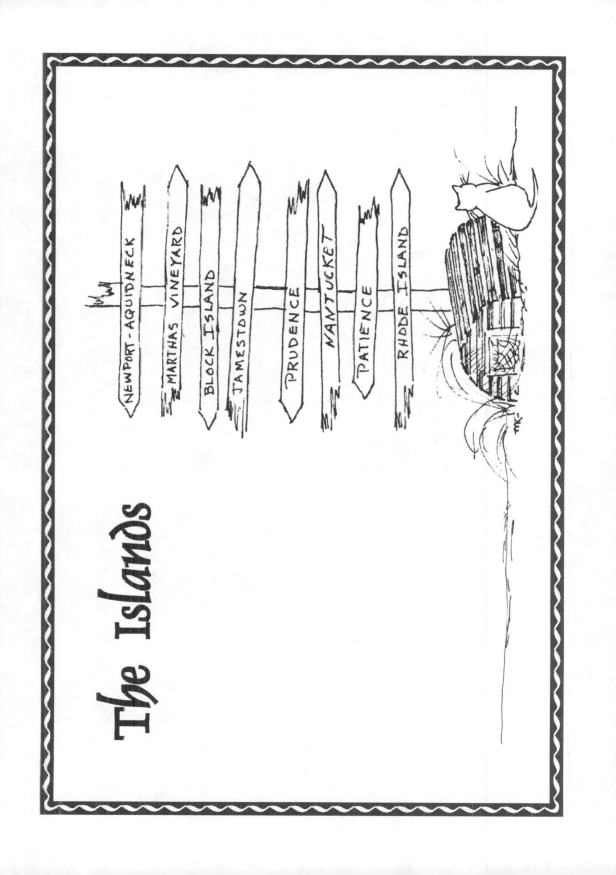

The Islands

Newport - Aquidneck
Marthas Vineyard
Block Island
Jamestown
Prudence
Nantucket
Patience
Rhode Island

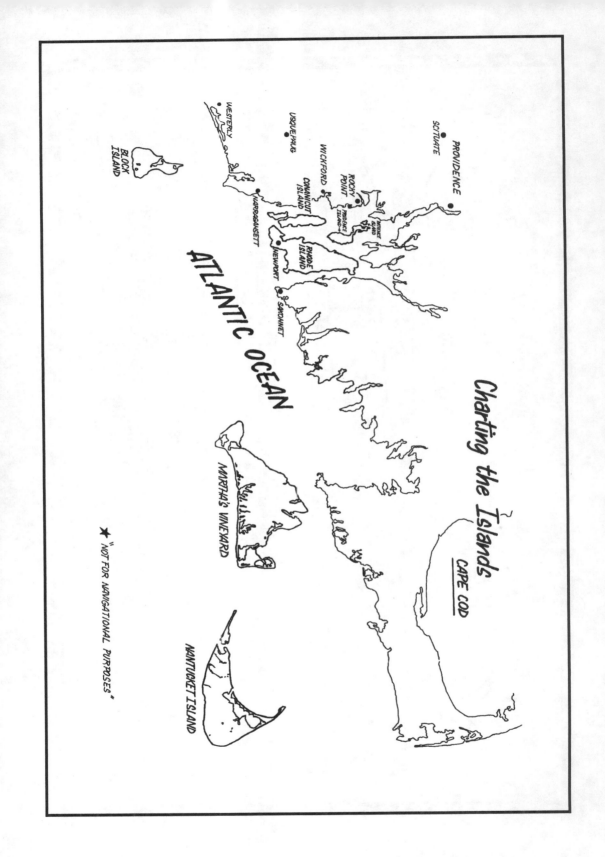

Charting the Islands

CAPE COD

ATLANTIC OCEAN

PROVIDENCE

SCITUATE

WESTERLY

USQUEPAUG

WICKFORD

ROCKY POINT

CONANICUT ISLAND

PRUDENCE ISLAND

PATIENCE ISLAND

BLOCK ISLAND

NARRAGANSETT

NEWPORT

RHODE ISLAND

SAKONNET

MARTHA'S VINEYARD

NANTUCKET ISLAND

★ "NOT FOR NAVIGATIONAL PURPOSES"

If once you have slept on an island
You'll never be quite the same!
You may look as you looked the day before
And go by the same old name.

You may bustle about in street and shop
You may sit at home and sew;
But you'll see blue water and wheeling gulls
Wherever your feet may go.

You may chat with the neighbors of this and that,
And close to your fire keep,
But you'll hear ships' whistles and lighthouse bells,
And tides beat through your sleep.

Oh but you won't know why and can't say when
Such change upon you came,
But—once you have slept on an island—
You'll never be quite the same!

Author Unknown

Taken from: Island Voices—Rhode Island's Islands Oral History, Summer 1986

I slands have a uniqueness of their own, and if you have ever visited one, or lived on one you will know what I mean. Each island has its own personality, as you will see from the description of their history and progress. They share "long winters of solitude" and the "fair days of summer" when the population swells. Surviving winter on an island can be an ordeal for those who require some interest beyond themselves and their families. Don't think islanders are "alone." A complete community in its own right, each island has its share of natives and "off-islanders" who determine their own destiny. Many activities range from informal gatherings with friends, to meeting at the post office each day, to church, school, libraries, historical societies, volunteer fire barns, the grocery store, et cetera. There is much to do in "the off season." Island residents look forward to this time of year.

The islands have one thing in common: each is "a far-away place." This book is an attempt to bring the islands closer together through time and the association of dining customs. Food is not only a necessity but a cultural and social experience. It reflects the heritage and travels of those who live there. In this day and age, nothing seems too far away, because of changes in transportation and engineering. "By land or by sea" is now the watchword for those traveling to and from the islands as "islanders" or tourists—by water in earlier days of canoes and packets and later "the ferries," and last but not least, the bridges. There still remain stretches of untouched beaches, bluffs, moors, wetlands and forests. Each person who comes in touch with the islands feels a sense of beauty and tranquility. Islands still make you feel as if "you've gotten away from it all," one of the reasons for the popularity and interest by "islanders" and tourists alike. Although many areas have lost some of their charm and history—they are different from the "mainland." I hope you will enjoy your trip to the Islands with us!

Rhode Island (Aquidneck Island) and Providence Plantations

Newport

The descriptions in the logs and journals of Verrazzano support the belief that he was the first white man to visit this area. In 1524, he referred to it as the Isle of Rhodes after the Greek island of Rhodes. Early records of this area indicate that the first inhabitants were Narragansetts, with a population estimated at about 30,000, about 5,000 of whom were warriors. Other tribes in the area included the Niantics, the Pequots, the Algonquins and the Wampanaugs. Wampanoag country extended from Narragansett Bay to Cape Cod Bay in 1620. By 1661, when Massoit died, the Indian lands had been reduced to Mount Hope Nec, Tiverton and Sakonnet, although on the west side of the Bay much was still held by the Narragansetts. During this time the Niantics merged with the Narragansetts in South County.

Providence Plantations was settled in June 1636 by Roger Williams, who had been forced to leave the Massachusetts Bay Colony for religious reasons. He called the farming community he established "Providence Plantations." His belief was that through "providence" he was able to settle there. He also believed that ownership was by possession, not by Royal Grant. Having purchased the Providence lands from the Narragansett Indians, he became very friendly with the Indians, a great boon to him and his followers because they had much to learn about the land.

The island was divided into 3 areas. Pocasset (now known as Portsmouth) to the North was settled in 1638. In the spring of 1639, a small group of men led by Coddington and Clarke founded Newport on the southern coast. Williams helped them purchase "Rhode Island" from the Indians. Middletown derives its name from its location; it was a part of the Newport Plantation until its incorporation in August 1743. It has remained an agricultural community, whereas Newport has become more urbanized. Now that I have you completely

confused about Rhode Island, we will clear things up about "Rhode Island" and Providence Plantations.

The Royal Charter of 1644 established the political relationship between the new colony of Rhode Island and the British Crown. This charter included the settlement at Newport, known as Rhode Island; hence the legal name of the state became Rhode Island and Providence Plantations. The area of Portsmouth, Middletown and Newport then became known as Aquidneck Island.

Those who lived in Providence Plantations were never really considered islanders, but their proximity to, and daily business with, the shore communities for fishing and commerce gave their lives much the same flavor as that of islanders. Narragansett Bay from the earliest days was the "Main Highway" in the area from Narragansett to Newport, from Prudence Island to Rocky Point, from South County to Jamestown and Newport, from Providence to Block Island, etc.

In early days another nickname for Rhode Island was "the Isle of Rogues," in reference to the pirates and slave traders. The name still seems appropriate today. Rhode Island probably has a more "bizarre and incredible" history than any other state. It was home to a diverse population, ranging from "free thinkers" to pirates. Some of the bloodiest battles of the Revolution and of King Phillip's War were fought on its soil.

Rhode Island was recognized as a haven for religious freedom. In 1638 the First Baptist Church of America was established in Providence. The first Quakers established a religious group around 1656. They were followed by the Congregational Church of Barrington in 1660, the Jewish Turo Synagogue in the 1650s, Trinity Church Newport-Episcopal in 1698, and in 1780 the first celebration of Roman Catholic Mass.

In 1709 the Narragansett Indian Reservation was established in Charlestown, which is part of South County. Currently, the Narragansett Reservation is trying to reclaim lands and status in Rhode Island. Their influence on farming and eating habits which can be traced as far back as the time of Roger Williams, is a legacy for which we can thank them. They introduced crops such as corn, squash and beans. Indian women were clever in combining plain cornmeal with raisins, wild fruits and nuts; these are the original counterparts of today's nut breads, blueberry muffins and raisin cookies, called dainties. The first strawberry bread or shortcake was a product of Indians' "bruising" the fruit and serving it with a sweet bread. "Hurtleberries" (huckleberries or blueberries) were dried and when beaten to a powder and mixed with meal were nearly as sweet as plum or spice cake. Wild turkey and other fowl were in abundance. Flint corn was destined to become the "stuff and substance" of jonnycakes. Native Indian foods comprised a major portion of New England fare. Cornmeal was a staple traveling food, used for cornmeal mush, Indian pudding and jonny-cakes. Other culinary favorites of Indian origin are traditional New England dishes such as succotash, strawberry shortcake, clam chowder and the ever-popular Rhode Island Clambake and Shore Dinner.

Narragansett "planters" had large estates that they called plantations on both sides of the bay. Rhode Island became famous for its development of "The Narragansett Pacer," the Rhode Island Red chicken in Little Compton and the Rhode Island Greening apple. Historically and economically, apples have played a leading role in the state's horticulture, as they continue to do even today. The first cider mill operated in 1743. Cider was reported in varying degrees of hardness, even though Apple Brandy was not mentioned. Large dairy herds were found throughout Rhode Island, with most of the milk being used for cheese and butter. As early as 1790 at the Philadelphia Society for the Promotion of Agriculture, top prizes were awarded for Rhode Island cheese. Pigs and pork were always popular as fresh tenderloins and chops, spareribs, head cheese, scrapple and mincemeat. From cattle much was mentioned of corned beef and smoked beef. Large farms in South County, which isn't really a county at all, developed many types of products. A fishing community in Gailee and Point Judith has Rhode Island's largest fishing cooperative.

With Rhode Island's 400-mile coastline, the tourist trade also has flourished on both sides of the bay. The east coast has become a haven for beach goers. It was known as the playground of New England, with its summer cottages in Narragansett, Watch Hill and Newport. The most prestigious address, of course, was Newport, on the Avenue where the Vanderbilts, the Astors and others had such famous "cottages" as the "Breakers" and "the Marble House," both of which are now kept open to the public by the Newport Preservation Society. After three and one-half centuries, Rhode Island still is known as "America's First Resort," with tremendous pride in its fine food, living history and international heritage. Besides sharing our coastline, parades, battle enactments, ethnic festivals, fairs, clambakes and international sporting events number among our many attractions. Come to the "Isle of Rogues" and play!

Block Island

A Visit to Another Time and Place

Old Harbor

Only 12 miles south of the mainland—and reached by ferry from Point Judith, Newport, New London and Providence— Block Island is almost as unspoiled as it was 100 years ago. Shaped like "a teardrop," the island is 7 miles long and 3 miles wide (a little less than 11 square miles). Block Island was originally inhabited by a tribe of Indians who called it "Manisses" or "Isle of the Little God." In 1524, on his way to what he hoped was Asia, the Italian explorer Verrazano spied the small island and called it "Claudia" in honor of the mother of the French king under whose flag he sailed. But the name by which it eventually became known was in honor of Adriaen Block, a Dutch navigator who in 1614 charted the island's location and named it "Adriaen's Eylant." Purchased and occupied in 1661, it was admitted to the colony as Block Island May 4, 1664. When it was incorporated on November 6, 1672, the name was changed to New Shoreham, "as signs of our unity, and likeness to many parts of our native country." Hundreds of fresh-water ponds, gently rolling hillsides, and stone walls cover what in earlier days was lush farmland. Resorts started to spring up in the mid-1800s. When transportation improved and the economy prospered, many vacationers visited the island. The 1938 hurricane and World War II caused the disappearance of nearly all the farmlands due to lack of manpower and the destruction by the hurricane. The fishing fleet was destroyed, and many families moved to Newport and Point Judith in Narragansett.

The island no longer enjoys an isolated lifestyle because of its easy access to the mainland, but island life in the off season still flourishes. Revealing the charm and closeness of the population are such social events as the local graduation exercises, autumn Roll Call Dinners popular since the early 1900s, the yearly Census on Ground Hog Day at a local inn, and the famous Corn Beef Dinner

Conanicut Island and Jamestown

Stepping Stone to Newport

Jamestown

Conanicut Island was purchased from the Narragansett Indians on April 1, 1657 by William Coddington, Benedict Arnold and others. They purchased it not only to have a stopping place on the way to the mainland, but as a real estate investment, which certainly was an interesting one for that time. Farms cropped up over the entire island and, because of fertile soil and a milder climate, the island prospered. Not much has been recorded about the early days of Conanicut, and a fire in latter years destroyed much of its historical documentation. Jamestown, the only town on Conanicut, was named for James I.

Water never really protected Conanicut from outside encroachment. Long before English settlers arrived, near the time of the last ice age, the sea level was lower. Original inhabitants could walk from

Other highlights of the island include the quaint architecture that is "vintage Victorian." For those who enjoy lighthouses, the North Light at Sandy Point built in 1867 is being restored as a maritime museum. Along the Mohegan Trail leading to the Bluffs you will see the Southeast Light built in 1873; its flashing beacon still operates. Perched above the sea, this brick structure looks like a ginger-bread house. At the island's highest point you can see four states on a clear day. Once called "a little sunny spot," this island brings sunshine to all who visit it.

for charity. A year-round population of 836 was recorded in 1990. Fishing and tourism are the main industries now thriving.

It is pointed out in much of the island literature that Block Island is being kept as much a part of "open space" as possible. A vital link in the biological chain, the island provides nesting areas and a stopping place for many migrating species. Block Island has a strong zoning code, not only to protect the island "from outside influences," but also from the islanders themselves.

Fishing has always been a way of life for islanders and Block Islanders are no different. Large portions of the catch were sold in Newport, New York and Cape May. Probably the most well-known catch is the Block Island swordfish, which even to this day is a prize for any sport fisherman.

Block Island boasts two magnificent harbors: Old Harbor is home to the fishing fleet and ferry docks while New Harbor is a haven for digging some of Block Island's famous quahogs. You can dig by hand or by foot, but you do need a license from the police station.

Saunderstown (North Kingstown) to what is now Jamestown. In bygone days, "everyone hunted; it was a necessity." They hunted rabbits, pheasant and ducks and, for a 25-cent bounty, even crows (to keep them out of the corn).

When the West Passage of Narragansett Bay froze over many years ago, it provided a chance for adventure. The venturesome could skate from Jamestown to Wickford or even to Rocky Point, something few would venture to do these days.

Since the opening of a bridge in 1939 across the West Passage connecting Jamestown with the mainland, the question has risen as to "when is an island not an island?" With the bridge access the scene in Jamestown changed. A defense military installation was added. Fort Wetherill's purpose was to protect "the Bay" with anti-submarine and anti-boat nets strung across "the Bay." With the advent of the new bridge a way of life was gone. It was "the end of an era." Organizations which flourished because of the "island closeness" no longer have this membership; they are divided according to "year-round" or "summer people." A downtown landmark was Lyons Market located in the center of "Jimmytown." The market stocked "only the best" of groceries for the island, as did the Pinta family, with the best in fruits and vegetables.

The ferry was the lifeline connecting Jamestown to Newport for shopping purposes as well as for those attending high school at Rogers. It took about 30 minutes to ride across the East Passage to Newport. The last ferry trip across the East Passage was in 1969 when the Newport Bridge opened, connecting Conanicut and Aquidneck Islands. Now, in the summertime, it will take you more than a half hour to go across the entire island of Jamestown. So much for progress.

Jamestown, like most other towns in Rhode Island, has become a bedroom community for Providence and even Boston, but many summer cottages are still found in this island paradise. Picture a thriving island community, which could only be reached by ferry, claiming a year-round population of 378, a far cry from the 1990 figure of 4,999. The island still has 2 or 3 dairy herds and, of course, Hotchkiss Farm, still operating as it has since the Revolutionary War, featuring vegetables and flowers at its unique stand and signpost welcoming customers.

Fishing is now a sportsman's pastime, and a delightful bait and tackle shop on North Road called Zeek's Creek caters to the locals or to passersby with suggestions for "today's favorite fishing spot." If you don't want to fish, they generally have "the catch of the day," which means fresh blues, sword, tuna, lobster, crabs and other fish that is local.

If you happen to go through the center of Jamestown, don't miss the new playground next to the Atheneum, which won a National Prize for innovation and design. Although it is not pictured on a Rhode Island map, be sure when you cross the Newport Bridge to Newport, that you look south and to the sea and spot "The House on the Rock," probably the area's smallest inhabited island, which is part of Jamestown. By the way, if you haven't noticed, Jamestown is still an island physically and spiritually.

Prudence and Patience

There is strong evidence that the Wampanoag Indians inhabited Prudence and other islands on the east passage of Narragansett Bay prior to the Narragansett Indians, although it is noted that some 500 Narragansetts lived on Prudence and Patience before 1637. The Indian name for Prudence Island was Chippaquasett (there are 15 different spellings of this word). A possible meaning is "place of separation of the passage." Prudence Island lies just two miles across the East Passage from Portsmouth and four miles from Bristol, yet it seems a far distance from the outside world. It

is of irregular shape, being seven miles long and at its widest point a little more than a mile, and consists of approximately 4,000 acres which include one quarter swamp and marshland.
The highest point on the island is 180 feet.

Much smaller is Patience Island, which is about an eighth of a mile from Prudence. John Oldham, in about 1634, was the first white man to visit and trade on the island. He may have stayed there a short time because of weather conditions, but he never lived there.

Narragansett Chief Canonacus was so friendly with Roger Williams that he made a gift of these islands to Williams, who later named them Prudence, Patience and Hope. Williams needed money to finance a trip to England to obtain a Charter from Charles II granting Rhode Island as a separate colony, instead of a part of Massachusetts. So the islands were sold and Rhode Island became the 13th colony.

Prudence, founded in 1639, was annexed to Portsmouth in May, 1647.

Early farmers were specialists in raising sheep, as well as peaches, plums, apples, pears, wild grapes and berries. The fertile farmland produced quantities of Indian corn.
Early islanders mixed corn with rye to make flour for bread. Farmers were self-sufficient, being able to grow whatever they needed with little assistance from the mainland. Supplies of shellfish and seafood were practically unlimited. As early as 1746, ferry service from Prudence to Warwick Neck was recorded.

Wild blueberries, blackberries, huckleberries, raspberries, cranberries and grapes were there for the picking. During the Depression, many came to Prudence to pick blueberries, filling washtubs with berries to sell in the city.

In an interview with Evelyn Kaiman, a long-time friend, I found that at this time she was the last living person who was born on Patience Island. After having lived there for a few years, her family moved to Prudence, where her father, Nicholas Herlein, farmed and supplied much of the island with produce as well as trips to Rocky Point (Warwick Neck, across the Bay). In latter years, he ran the general store which was the hub of activity for the island for many years. Evelyn and her husband Sol later took over the general store and, from 1943 to 1954, Evelyn was a teacher on the island, with the exception of 3 years during that time. Prudence, she recalls, "was a great place to live, but an even better place to bring up your children." On Prudence you learn to make your own recreation—walking, sledding and skating on frozen ponds. Evelyn says.

Island natives still close to the soil, Natalie Chase Bacon and son Nat own and operate The Prudence Island Vineyard. The elder Mrs. Chase and Mrs. Herlein were excellent cooks,

The summer population can come close to 3,000 but the hearty year-rounders number between 60 and 70. The population in the winter seems to stay fairly constant with many retirees joining the ranks of the islanders. Why here? Many say it is a time to collect your thoughts. Isn't that what an island is for?

Martha's Vineyard

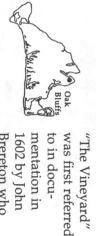

Oak Bluffs

"The Vineyard" was first referred to in documentation in 1602 by John Brereton who traveled with the English explorer, Gosnold. It is generally agreed that Gosnold named the island so lush with grapes in honor of his baby daughter Martha—thus the name Martha's Vineyard.

Seven miles at sea, this largest island in New England lies not too distant from Rhode Island and Southeast Massachusetts. Its unique sculpture from the ice age makes it unique in appearance. Early evidence of the ice age is the geological story told by the Gayhead Cliffs. Approximately 23 miles long and 9 miles wide, about 100 square miles, Martha's Vineyard contains one county, Dukes, and 6 towns. Referred to most often as "down island," the easterly side of the island contains the most populated towns of Tisbury (Vineyard Haven), Oak Bluffs, Edgartown (and Chappaquiddick,

which is really an island reached by a ferry from the town dock.) On the western side of the island are the towns of West Tisbury, Chilmark and Gayhead. Gayhead Light was one of the first revolving lights in the country. Other lighthouses include West Chop, East Chop, Edgartown and Cape Poge.

First inhabitants of the island were Indians who may have been here as long as 5000 years ago. The Indians were Wampanoags, which translated means "easterners." "Gayhead Indians," as they were called, showed early settlers how to master the sea and its creatures. The art of launching open boats and capturing whales just offshore must have been a sight to see. The settlers learned how to plant corn, dry and smoke fish, harvest the cranberries and learned the secret of "alewives in the spring." The first Gayhead Indian to attend Harvard did so in 1665.

Still a viable group, the Wampanoag Tribe of Gayhead (Aquinnah) is a popularly-elected tribe with a tribal government. In 1987, an act PL95-100, a land claim settlement, changed the tribe's focus. The settlement includes the face of Gayhead Cliffs, Hurry Creek and the Cranberry Bogs. Major projects that the tribe is pursuing include a tribal multipurpose building, a tribal museum and archives, a fine arts center, tribal resort complex and a tribal history project.

Much regional recorded history can be seen in collections at the Seamen's Bethel, The D.A.R. Historical Museum and other local museums. Vineyard Haven was at one time a booming seaport where deepwater vessels, as well as schooners, arrived for services of all kinds. When the Cape Cod Canal opened in 1914, the advent of steamships and changes in mass transportation caused maintenance commerce in this port to dwindle. As also happened in Nantucket, "The Great Fire" of 1883 nearly wiped out the center of town.

Oak Bluffs, called Cottage City until 1907, was recognized as the first summer resort. A religious insurgence by Baptists and Methodists alike brought people from far and wide to the Wesleyan Camp Grove started in 1835. Ministers with great "fervor and zeal" brought many to the island to "be saved." Many attending the "camp meetings" decided to stay on after the meetings and built permanent cottages of rococo design with high-pitched roofs, verandas, excessive scrollwork, and in many colors. Today this popular part of the island is still inhabited by "year-rounders." The porches continue to be one of the big attractions with their "Hansel and Gretel era" architecture. The "gingerbread houses" in Ocean Park, larger than those around the campground, have patterned shingles and the site has an octagonal bandstand. An attraction not to be missed is the "Flying Horses," one of the oldest merry-go-rounds in the United States.

In the West Tisbury locale, once the site of many sheep farms, are the Chicamo Vineyards on Stoney Hill Road. A large farmers' market, open during the summer season, offers fruits of the farm and the sea available from local entrepreneurs, including jams, jellies, salsa, smoked bluefish, and many other delicious surprises. The area's State Lobster Hatchery, which is open to the public, has a unique way of "helping nature along," the Hatchery's main accomplishment. Much research has been done in the working laboratory on the living habits of crustaceans. Egg-laden females are brought to the hatchery, where this unusual nursery provides a controlled and safe environment for young lobsters before they are released to the sea.

The "Vineyard Gazette" founded in 1846 is still going strong with two issues a week in summer and a weekly issue the rest of the year. Currently, ferries are operated from Woods Hole, Falmouth, New Bedford and Hyannis. Special festivals, only to mention a few, include Campground Community Sings every Wednesday, Band Concerts on Sunday, The Wampanoags Cranberry Feast, Martha's Vineyard Livestock Show and Fair, Striped Bass and Bluefish Derby, Happy Haunting Weekend in October and, last but not least, "Whale of a Christmas," which lasts the entire month of December.

As of the 1990 Census, Martha's Vineyard tallied 11,541 year-round residents, while the summer influx brings on approximately 94,708 persons. Who says that islands aren't changeable?

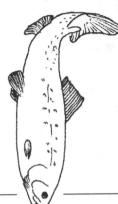

Nantucket— The Far-Away Island

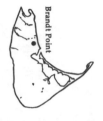

Brandt Point

The name Nantucket was taken from the Indian word Nanticut, meaning "The Far Away Land," because it is 30 miles from the mainland. At the beginning of the 17th century this "far-away" island was inhabited by about 2,500 Indians living at either end of the island. Those on the easterly end are believed to have come from the Cape and those on the westerly end and from the Vineyard. Both groups spoke the Algonquin language. Feasts, when the men returned from hunting and fishing trips, consisted of shellfish the women prepared, deer and sometimes corn and beans, which were the mainstay of their diet. Meals were cooked on sticks in the center of their wigwams.

Nantucket Island was granted to the Plymouth Company by the British Crown in 1621. An Englishman from the Massachusetts Bay Colony,

Thomas Mayhew, settled the Island in 1659. The island belonged to the province of New York before it became part of Massachusetts. Before the Revolutionary War, Nantucket was one of the great whaling centers of the world. As many as 125 whaling ships had their home port there. For a century and a half Nantucket remained one of the busiest and most prosperous whaling ports of the world. In the early 1800s, as a port of call for transatlantic "packets," it ranked only after New York, Boston and Salem harbors in size.

As in Jamestown, Prudence and "Rhode Island," grist mills were in great use until the turn of the century; islanders depended on their own supplies of meal. The first smoking of bluefish was attributed to the Indians of Nantucket. Other shellfish and fish they harvested were Tuckernuck mussels, striped bass, littlenecks, cherrystones, quahogs, and Nantucket Bay scallops, which today cannot be harvested between March 31 and October 1, and require permits to do so in season.

In the 1800s, "the great hotels" flourished because of New York and

Boston people who wanted fresh air, good food and an escape from the hustle and bustle of urban life. The island economy grew by leaps and bounds.

In early days, sheep farming was most important. Around the 1830s, with as many as 9,000 to 10,000 sheep on the islands, "the sheep shearing festival" became a great economic effort and a social event as well. Everyone who attended brought food;

"pigs were roasted whole; there were ham, hard-boiled eggs, cakes of all kinds, oysters, spruce beer and lemonade." Cranberries which were very plentiful, were used not only for food, but as effective treatment for sores and wounds.

Because of its reputation as "the Atlantic Graveyard," Nantucket has done its best to warn seafarers of the rocky shoals in the area with

lighthouses. They include Great Point, built in 1784; Brandt Point, built in 1846 at the harbor; and Sankaty Head on the eastern shore, which soon joins the ranks of "the must-be-moved." Hurricanes and heavy coastal storms have destroyed the bluff on this side of the Atlantic Ocean. A local sign in Sconset says, "3,000 miles to Spain."

It is easy to see why the island is referred to as "The Little Grey Lady by the Sea" with its unique architecture of simple houses with greying, weather-beaten shingles. You will also see grand whaling captains' homes with "widows' walks" and Federal period homes. Another uniqueness of Nantucket is its climbing roses, seen over picket fences, in arbors, rambling over roofs, just everywhere in deep pinks or reds in June and July. The most popular is the "Dorothy Perkins" rose.

Nantucket has changed little in its appearance over the past century, although automobiles, mopeds and bicycles today blur the scene. Nantucket Town's Main Street of cobblestones is a colorful sight no matter what season. One of the charms of a summer's morn are the flowers, herbs and vegetables for sale at the farm wagons drawn up at "The Hub." One thing is for sure: Nantucket has always been known for having some of the best kitchens in the country, whether in a Quaker household, a whaling master's quarters or a country inn, the food on Nantucket excels. Try some local honey, which is available in fine gift shops, specialty food stores and farm stands throughout the island. Unsurpassed in flavor is cranberry honey. Remember the largest single bog in the world is in Nantucket. Probably the "best scallops" in the world come from Nantucket; they are even "sweeter than honey."

In the harbor, you will hear the moan of the foghorn and see the ferries arriving with their "daytrippers" and supplies for the island. Snuggled into Straight Wharf are small fishing boats, pleasure yachts, sailboats and dinghies and sometimes even a giant cruise ship. How things have changed from the whaling days. There is always something to do in Nantucket—from the Daffodil Festival the last weekend in April, to "sand-castle contests," flower and antique shows, all leading up to the grand finale, "The Christmas Stroll," when the whole island is dressed up and has open house "for the season." Once you have been on an island such as this, you will return again and again.

Wetting Your Whistle
and So Forth

Gil's Bloody Mary Mix

One of the greatest drinks ever, found at the famous Jared Coffin House—even without vodka

4 ounces heavy tomato juice
Juice from 1/4 lemon
1 tablespoon Worcestershire sauce
1 dash bitters
3 pinches celery salt
1/4 teaspoon extra fine sugar
1/2 dash Tabasco sauce
1 1/2 ounces vodka

❖ Pour all ingredients over ice in a very large goblet and garnish with a slice of lime and a stalk of celery. Stir...do not shake.

Mock Champagne Cocktail

1 7-ounce bottle lemon-lime carbonated beverage, cold
1/2 cup apple juice chilled
3 thin slices lemon

❖ Just before serving, mix carbonated beverage and apple juice. Serve in stemmed glasses with lemon slice in each. Serve 3.

Eggnog for Those Who Shouldn't

Delicious even though it isn't the real thing and besides you won't have to worry about salmonella poisoning because the egg substitute is pasteurized.

2 cups skim milk
Egg substitute equal to 6 eggs
4 teaspoons vanilla
1/4 cup sugar
Rum or brandy, optional
Nutmeg

❖ Beat milk, egg substitute, vanilla and sugar together until frothy. Pour into chilled glasses. Add 1 ounce rum or brandy to taste.
Top with fresh ground nutmeg.

Fruit Quencher

1 cup seeded watermelon cubes
1 cup plain low-fat yogurt
1 6 1/2-ounce bottle sparkling water, chilled

❖ Using a blender or food processor, blend watermelon and yogurt until smooth. Add sparkling water and serve. Serves 2.

Frozen Fruit Ring

1 6-ounce can pink lemonade concentrate
1 quart ginger ale
1 29-ounce can fruit cocktail, drained
Mint or spearmint leaves

❖ Combine pink lemonade concentrate with ginger ale. Arrange a little fruit and mint leaves in bottom of 1 1/2 to 2-quart ring mold. Pour in a small amount of lemonade mixture. Freeze to set fruit. Add remaining ginger ale mixture, fruit cocktail and mint leaves. Freeze thoroughly. Unmold and float in punch.

Home Brew

Delicious after dinner

2 cups dried apricots
2 cups sugar
2 cups vodka

❖ Wash and dry the apricots. Dissolve the sugar in the vodka, (you can heat it, but make sure you do not boil) stir well. Put the apricots into a wide mouth bottle (half-gallon cider bottle) and pour the vodka mixture over them. Seal and store in a dark place for 2 months.

Orange Nectar

1/4 cup egg substitute
6 ounces orange juice
1/2 teaspoon sugar or substitute

❖ Put all ingredients into blender and beat on High. Pour over crushed ice. Makes 1 serving.

Cranberry Apple Punch

3 quarts water
2 cups sugar
2 cups strong tea
2 6-ounce cans frozen lemonade
2 quarts cranberry juice
1 quart apple juice
2 cups orange juice

❖ Heat water and sugar to boiling, stirring constantly until sugar is dissolved. Cool. Prepare tea; cool. Chill all ingredients. Just before serving, stir together in large punch bowl. Makes 60 servings.

Mocha Punch

1 cup sugar
2 quarts strong coffee
1 quart chocolate ice cream
1 quart vanilla ice cream
Whipped cream

❖ Add sugar to hot coffee and cool. Spoon ice cream into coffee. Fold in whipped cream. Serves about 25 using punch cups.

Vineyard Haven Planter's Punch

The first time I went to Martha's Vineyard, I was introduced to this refreshing cooler. We rented bicycles. The first mile I thought I'd just about make it; the second mile I thought I'd die; and the third mile I thought I was dying until I pleaded we stop for a drink of water. Instead, I was introduced to this refresher! Well, as the story goes, I rode another 5.6 miles with no problem, except an unbelievable sunburn.

Juice of 1 lime
Juice of 1/2 lemon
Juice of 1/2 orange
1 teaspoon pineapple juice
1 teaspoon grenadine
2 ounces imported rum

❖ Fill a 16-ounce glass with shaved ice. Pour all ingredients over ice. Stir until glass is frosted, then add 1 ounce Jamaican rum and top with 1/4 teaspoon Curaçao. Garnish with slice of orange, lemon, pineapple and a cherry. Serve with straws.

Providence Punch

From the Providence Athenaeum, historic landmark, library, cultural center and literary haunt for over two and a quarter centuries and known for its "literary" cookbooks, this recipe is an adaptation of the original.

1 cup strong cold tea
Juice of ½ lemon
1 teaspoon sugar
Champagne or other bubbly (there are many delicious non-alcoholic fruit flavors)
Crushed ice

❖ Pour tea into a large goblet. Add lemon juice and sugar. Stir well. Add bubbly and fill glass with crushed ice.

Rum Punch

2 quarts ginger ale
2 quarts cranberry juice
2 pints orange sherbet
1 quart light rum

❖ Refrigerate ginger ale and cranberry juice. Place sherbet in punch bowl; pour rum, ginger ale and cranberry juice over sherbet.

Shirley's Rum Punch

1   46-ounce can pineapple juice
3 cups apricot nectar
1 quart ginger ale
1 quart pineapple or orange sherbet
Rum to taste

❖ Mix together pineapple juice, apricot nectar and ginger ale in a large punch bowl. Just before serving, add the sherbet and rum.

❖ Note: May omit the rum.

Strawberry Punch

❖ Cook 1 quart mashed strawberries with 1½ cups sugar and ½ cup water until berries are soft. Strain the mixture. Add juice of 1 lemon to the syrup. Bring to a boil and dilute with water for use.

Coffee

If you haven't noticed, "The Islands" have coffee—everything from Iced Coffee to Coffee Cabinets. When you visit other parts of the country, you soon realize that you come from "another world"....Coffeeland. Eclipse and Autocrat have not left the area in most cases, except by special request of family and friends who have moved from the area. Recently the two companies merged but the two products are still being marketed under those names in pint and even in gallon sizes.

Tokyo Fog

1 quart bourbon
1 quart extra-strength coffee, cooled
1 quart vanilla ice cream

❖ Combine ingredients in bowl and beat until smooth. Refrigerate until serving time. May be served from small punch bowl into cocktail glasses or punch cups. Makes about 20 (4-ounce) servings.

Leftover Coffee

And now the leftover coffee. Heaven forbid if you throw it out...Yankees were noted for being frugal and not wasting— "Waste not want not" was one of their themes. Try Coffee Jelly, page 145 and Coffee Ice Cream, page 141.

❖ **RI's Official Drink (Coffee Milk):** Take an 8-ounce glass of milk and add whatever amount you want of coffee syrup and stir.

Coffee Shake: Take an 8-ounce glass of milk and 1/4 cup coffee syrup and mix until frothy in blender.

Coffee Cabinet: (Frappe, Frosty etc.) Take 8 ounces of whole milk, 2 generous scoops Coffee Ice Cream and about 1/4 cup coffee syrup. Beat in blender until thick and creamy.

The Opera House

Of all of the old-time haunts of Nantucket Island, The Opera House was probably one of the finest. Many an hour was passed sipping this famous Nantucket coffee on South Water Street.

Opera House Coffee

❖ Fill a tall glass (at least 12 ounces) with ice cubes, then add 1½ ounces cognac and 1 ounce coffee-flavored liqueur. Top with extra strong coffee and stir well. Serve immediately with a straw. If you really want to go big time, add a dollop of whipped cream. Good winter or summer.

Iced Lemonade Tea

According to Larousse Gastronomique, "barley water is made by boiling 2 teaspoons Pearl barley, washed in cold water, until completely cooked in enough water to have 1 quart of liquid after boiling. Allow to stand for a moment and strain." A popular medicine used by Hippocrates.

6 tea bags
1 quart barley water
1 6-ounce can frozen lemonade
2 quarts ice water
1/4 cup sugar

❖ Steep tea bags in boiling barley water for 15 minutes. Add

lemonade concentrate; stir until melted. Stir in cold water and sugar until sugar is dissolved. Chill. Serve on ice. Makes 12 (8-ounce) servings.

Russian Tea

1 cup Tang
1 cup sugar
1/3 cup instant tea
1 teaspoon cinnamon
1/2 teaspoon ground cloves

❖ Mix ingredients thoroughly and store in a tightly covered jar. Mix 1 to 2 teaspoons per cup of boiling water.

Spiced Apple Party Mix

1/2 teaspoon ground cinnamon
1/4 teaspoon ground nutmeg
1 cup raisins
3/4 cup coarsely chopped dried apples
1 cup walnut pieces

❖ In medium bowl, combine cinnamon and nutmeg. Add raisins and apples; toss to coat with spices. Add walnuts and toss. Store in airtight container. Makes 2½ cups.

Brie in Pastry

1 sheet Pepperidge Farm frozen puff pastry
1 16-ounce wheel Brie cheese
1/4 cup sliced toasted almonds
1/4 cup parsley, chopped
1 egg, beaten with 1 teaspoon water

❖ Thaw pastry 20 minutes. Roll out sheet on lightly floured surface to a 15-inch circle. Preheat oven to 400° F. Slice Brie in half horizontally and layer with almonds and parsley. Reassemble and place in center of pastry. Brush pastry edges with egg wash, and pull up sides to enclose Brie. Place seam side down on ungreased baking sheet. Brush with egg wash. Bake for 20 minutes. Let stand for 10 minutes before serving. Makes 12 servings.

Warmed Cranberry Brie

1/3 cup crushed cranberry sauce
2 tablespoons packed brown sugar
1/4 teaspoon rum extract
1/8 teaspoon chopped nutmeg
1 8-ounce Brie cheese
2 tablespoons chopped pecans

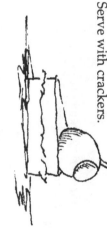

❖ Combine cranberry sauce, brown sugar, rum extract and nutmeg. Peel off top rind of Brie cheese, leaving 1/4-inch rim. Top Brie with cranberry mixture and sprinkle with chopped pecans. Bake at 500° F for 4 to 5 minutes. Serve with assorted crackers.

Mock Boursin Cheese

3 8-ounce packages cream cheese
1/4 pound margarine
1 8-ounce jar Green Goddess salad dressing
Pepper
Minced garlic

❖ Blend together softened cream cheese and margarine. Add remainder of ingredients and mix well. Refrigerate for at least 2 hours. Serve with crackers.

Cheese Biscuits

1/2 pound butter, softened
1/2 pound grated Cheddar cheese
3 cups sifted flour
1 8-ounce can Parmesan cheese
Dash of cayenne pepper

❖ Cream butter and cheese together until smooth. Work in flour, Parmesan cheese and cayenne pepper. Shape into small balls or roll and cut. Bake at 350° F until brown. Cool. Dust with powdered sugar (optional).

Jane's Pini Cheese

A great gift item for a harried hostess...(I should know, since Jane brought me her favorite recipe all prepared for a surprise birthday party for my husband.)

1 8-ounce package cream cheese
3 ounces Roquefort cheese
1 tablespoon chopped pimento
10 sliced pistachio nuts

❖ Beat all ingredients with mixer until well blended. Should be made at least a day before serving. Serve with crackers of your choice.

Clams Casino

12 Little Neck clams
1 green pepper
Garlic powder
Cayenne red pepper
2 slices bacon

❖ Open clams and leave on the half shell, being careful not to lose the juice. Put a small piece of green pepper on top of opened clam and sprinkle lightly with garlic powder and cayenne. Put a small piece of bacon, enough to almost cover, on each clam. Place clams in a metal baking platter and broil for 2 to 3 minutes, just until bacon is done. Serve immediately.

Baked Stuffed Quahogs

❖ Use quahogs only if alive and full of juice. Open quahogs, put juice and clams in bowl. Make coarse bread crumbs, toasted. Put quahogs and juice in blender or food processor, chop just a little. Add a small amount of garlic powder, sweet basil and chopped onion (not too much of any). Place a little butter in

each shell, then clam mixture, then bread crumbs, top with a piece of bacon. Sprinkle with cayenne red pepper and paprika. Bake at 350° F for about 30 minutes.

Zucchini Onion Dip

One of the persons who encouraged me to write this cookbook is a Long Island lady named Millie Delahunty, Certified Home Economist. Her greeting to me has been, "Well, when are you going to write it?" She specializes in microwave cooking education and communication. Her microwave cooking school, television appearances in the New York area, and, her internationally sold texts on microwaving make her an expert in this area. Thanks, Millie, for your help in thinking this project through as well as for this simple and easy recipe for the microwave.

2 teaspoons vegetable oil
1/2 cup chopped onion
1 clove garlic, halved
2 cups chopped zucchini
1 teaspoon salt
Dash each of pepper and lemon juice
1/2 cup plain low-fat yogurt

❖ Put oil, onion, garlic and zucchini in 1-quart bowl. Cover with vented plastic wrap. Heat at High (100%) power for 4 to 5 minutes, stirring once. Add salt, pepper and lemon juice. Process with steel blade in food processor until puréed. Pour into serving bowl; stir in yogurt. Serve at room temperature or chilled, with crackers.

Slim Deviled Eggs

6 hard-cooked eggs, peeled and cut into halves lengthwise
3 tablespoons plain yogurt
2 teaspoons prepared mustard
1/2 teaspoon dill
Dash of salt and pepper
1 teaspoon grated orange peel

❖ Carefully remove egg yolks from whites and mash thoroughly in a bowl. Add remaining ingredients and mix well until creamy.

❖ Mound mixture in each egg white shell. Garnish with paprika or cayenne red pepper. Refrigerate until serving time.

Scotch Eggs

For a nifty snack or appetizer

❖ Roll some bulk pork sausage around peeled, hard-cooked eggs, dip in beaten egg and bread crumbs. Fry in a skillet or deep-fat fryer. They're good hot or cold.

Grandma Zarli's Fritter Batter

1 egg, beaten
1 cup flour
1 teaspoon baking powder
1 teaspoon salt
3/4 cup liquid or milk

❖ Beat egg in a medium bowl and lightly fold in flour, baking powder, salt and liquid.

❖ Can be used for clam, corn or fruit fritters. If making clam fritters, use clam juice combined with milk.

❖ Add 1/2 to 1 cup chopped clams, corn or fruit—apple, peach, etc. Fry in hot fat in a heavy frying pan until first side is lightly browned and fritter starts to puff, turn and cook until brown on other side.

❖ Drain on paper towel. Serve immediately.

❖ Note: Do not pat or play with fritter while cooking.

Barbara's Stuffed Mushrooms

This recipe originated out of pure laziness by the author. Many of my friends had given me recipes for stuffed mushrooms and either I didn't feel like that much work. Well, necessity is the mother of invention, and I had been asked to have Stuffed Mushrooms by a particular individual who was coming to dinner. I'm sure there are a few products in the marketplace which I could sell with no problem at all and one of them is Pepperidge Farm Stuffing Mix... I use it for everything. Get ready, it's simple and easy!

1 pound fresh mushrooms, at least
  1 inch in diameter
Salt and pepper
Garlic powder
2 cups stuffing mix
1/2 cup margarine
Hot water

❖ Wipe mushrooms with a paper towel. Remove stems and put in food processor or chop very fine with knife. Add a small amount of salt, pepper and garlic powder to mushrooms, stuffing mix and 1/4 cup margarine. Mix well. Add just enough hot water in bowl so that ingredients will stick together. Put mushroom caps in a baking pan with hollow side up. Cut remaining margarine into small pieces and put 1 piece in each cap. Mound a teaspoonful of filling into cap, pressing mixture together so it will stay together. Bake, uncovered, at 350° F for about 20 minutes.

❖ Serve immediately. They'll disappear like potato chips and the next time you invite these same guests they'll tell you, "We're not coming if you're not making mushrooms."

❖ Note: This may be made ahead and kept in the freezer for 2 to 3 weeks. I made 20 pounds of these for my daughter's PhD party, since time saving was important.

Lambert's Stuffed Mushrooms

1/2 pound Gorgonzola cheese
1/2 cup butter, softened
2 tablespoons minced fresh parsley
1/2 cup chopped walnuts
30 medium fresh mushroom caps

❖ Cream together the Gorgonzola cheese and butter. Add the parsley and walnuts. Remove the stems from the mushrooms, wipe caps clean with a paper towel. Mound the cheese mixture by small spoonfuls on the mushroom caps. Chill, tightly covered, until serving time.

Potato Sticks with Cheese-Bacon-Onion Dip

A lot of work but worth it!

3 cups flour, divided
1 package dry yeast
1/4 cup sugar
1 teaspoon salt
1/2 cup mashed potato
1/2 cup milk
1/4 cup butter, melted
1 egg, beaten
Coarse salt, optional
Cheese Bacon Onion Dip

❖ Combine 1 1/2 cups flour, yeast, sugar, and salt in large mixing bowl; set aside.

❖ Heat potato, milk and butter until warm (110° F). Add to flour mixture; blend well. Add egg; beat with mixer 3 minutes at medium speed. Gradually add remaining flour to make firm dough.

❖ Knead 3 to 5 minutes or until smooth and elastic. Place in greased bowl; turn to grease top. Let rise, covered, in warm place for 15 minutes. Punch dough down.

❖ On floured surface, roll dough into 12x9-inch rectangle. Cut dough into twenty-four 9x1/2-inch strips, cut each strip in half crosswise. Twist strips; roll in coarse salt, if desired. Place twists on greased cookie sheet about 3/4 inch apart.

❖ Bake at 400° F for 10 to 15 minutes or until golden brown.

❖ Cool slightly; serve warm with Cheese-Bacon-Onion Dip. Makes about 48 sticks.

❖ Note: For mashed potato, wash potato, prick skin and microwave on High for about 4 minutes. Allow to stand 3 to 5 minutes. Cut open; remove potato and mash.

Cheese-Bacon-Onion Dip

1 8-ounce package softened cream cheese
1/2 cup shredded Cheddar cheese
2 tablespoons crumbled cooked bacon or substitute
2 tablespoons chopped green onion

❖ Combine all ingredients and blend thoroughly. Makes about 1 cup.

Sesame Seed Sticks

1 recipe 8 or 9-inch pastry
1/2 cup sesame seed
1 tablespoon butter or margarine

❖ Roll out the pastry into an oblong about 1/4 inch thick. Dot with butter. Fold, turn and roll out again. Sprinkle with sesame seed. Cut into 24 strips. Bake at 350° F for 5 minutes, then reduce heat to 325° F until delicately brown.

Parmesan Puffs

3 ounces cream cheese
1 cup mayonnaise
1½ teaspoons grated onion
1/3 cup grated Parmesan cheese
1/8 teaspoon cayenne pepper
1 loaf thin sliced bread

❖ Mix together cream cheese, mayon-naise, onion, cheese and cayenne pepper. Cut 1 loaf of thin sliced bread in 2-inch rounds with a cookie cutter. Spread cheese mix-ture on bread rounds and put under broiler for only 1 to 2 minutes, only enough to melt and puff. Be careful not to burn. May be made before-hand and then popped into the oven.

Island Miniature Pizzas

10 ounces extra-sharp Cheddar cheese
1 medium onion, minced
1 6½-ounce can minced clams, drained
English muffins, split

❖ Grate Cheddar cheese; add onion and clams. Mix well. Spread English muffins with mixture. Put under broiler until bubbly. Cut into

eighths. These may be frozen and broiled when ready to use.

❖ Variation: Minced bacon or bacon bits may be substituted for clams.

Stuffed Cherry Tomatoes

2 6-ounce cans baby shrimp, drained well
1/4 cup mayonnaise
2 tablespoons sour cream
1 teaspoon curry powder
1/4 cup finely chopped celery
1/8 teaspoon salt
Pepper
20 good-sized cherry tomatoes

❖ Combine all ingredients, except tomatoes and mix well. Wash and dry tomatoes, then cut an X into the top of tomato removing stem. Pull back all 4 sections to resemble the petals of a flower. Fill each tomato with filling. Top each with a sprig of parsley. Refrigerate, covered with plastic wrap, until ready to serve. May substitute white tuna or crab meat for shrimp or use your favorite egg salad recipe.

Herb Cheese Walnuts

1/2 cup grated Parmesan cheese
1 teaspoon parsley flakes
1/2 teaspoon Italian herbs
1/2 teaspoon garlic salt
Dash of cayenne pepper
1 egg white
2 cups walnuts

❖ In medium bowl, combine cheese, parsley, herb seasoning, garlic salt and cayenne; set aside. In small bowl, beat egg white until frothy. Add walnuts; toss to coat. Stir walnuts into cheese mixture; mix thoroughly. Spread in single layer on lightly oiled baking sheet. Bake in preheated 250° F oven for about 30 minutes or until golden and crisp. Cool completely. Store in airtight container. Makes about 2 cups.

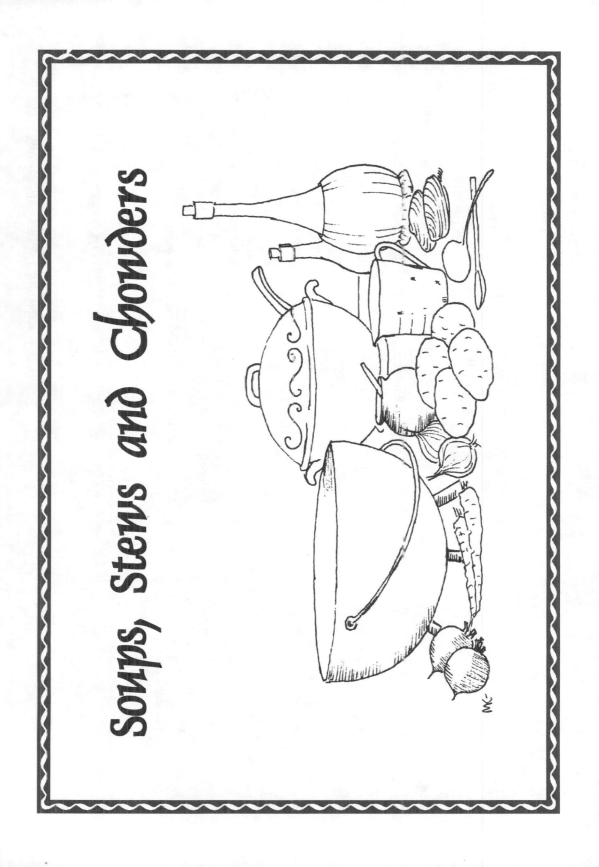

Soups, Stews and Chowders

Cherry Valley Herb Farm

Susan Morrison Carpenter is one of the many personalities who helped me with my "idea" but who represents "The Joy of Living." I have been acquainted with Susan for many years in our community through the famous Scituate Art Festival in which she has exhibited since her high school days. How I really got to know her was the year the teachers in our system decided we would "get in shape," and Susan and I became soulmates in "Weight Watchers at Work." Well, we watched and watched our weight, but our waists did not waste and we traded old time recipes and stories about food, herbs and gardening. Recently, Susan and her husband, Brian, bought and developed a delightful old farm in the hills of Gloucester and Cherry Valley Herb Farm emerged—as a real working farm, gift shop, workshop, showroom and school. Her love for food done simply with just a pinch of this and that and basic cooking techniques have earned her recognition as an herbalist

and cook. She is another Yankee who grew up with "soup and more"—Hope you enjoy her additions to this delicious collection of soups, stews and chowders.

Susan's Cream of Broccoli

4 bags frozen chopped broccoli
1 46-ounce can chicken broth
1 large onion, chopped
1 carrot, diced
1 potato, diced
Dry thyme or bay leaf

❖ Cook for 10 to 15 minutes in a heavy pan. Purée in blender and then pour into Pyrex bowl.

1/4 cup margarine (1 stick)
8 tablespoons flour
Dried mustard
Black pepper
3 to 4 cups whole milk

❖ Make a roux of margarine, flour, mustard, black pepper and milk for cream sauce. Mix with puréed broccoli mixture. Cheddar cheese may be used to garnish. Serve hot. May be frozen.

White Bean Soup

A quick, easy vegetarian soup

1 onion, finely chopped
2 carrots, finely chopped
1 teaspoon oil
2 16-ounce cans white beans (cannellini) undrained
2 chopped tomatoes

❖ Sauté onion and carrots in oil in a 2-quart saucepan until onion is soft. Add beans and tomatoes. Simmer 20 minutes. Add salt and pepper to taste and more water if needed.

Homemade Noodles

❖ Slightly beat 1 egg, add 1 tablespoon water, a sprinkle of salt and about 3/4 cup flour. Mix well with fork and add more flour if sticky. Knead on floured board until mixed. Roll out on floured board as thin as possible. Let dry, uncovered. Slice into noodles and toss with a little flour to keep from sticking. Let dry until ready to use.

Beef Noodle Soup

1 rib roast bone or 1 pound beef shin
1 onion, sliced
3 carrots, peeled
1 tablespoon chopped parsley
1/4 teaspoon thyme
6 cups water
3 beef bouillon cubes
1/2 cup green beans
1 rib celery, or chopped celery leaves
Wedge of cabbage
Homemade or packaged noodles
(see page 32)

❖ Put bone or beef shin into large
kettle. Add onion, 1 carrot, parsley,
thyme, water, bouillon cubes, salt
and pepper. Cover loosely and
simmer until meat is tender.

❖ Cut meat from bone and add to broth.

❖ Add remaining sliced carrots and
other vegetables. Simmer until
vegetables are tender.

❖ Add noodles and simmer until
cooked—about 10 to 12 minutes.

Cheese Soup with Rice

2 tablespoons butter
1 tablespoon chopped onion
2 tablespoons flour
2 cups milk
1 teaspoon salt
1/4 teaspoon pepper
1/2 to 1 cup grated Cheddar cheese
2 egg yolks, well beaten
1 1/2 cups cooked rice

❖ Melt butter in saucepan. Sauté
onion and then stir in flour. Slowly
add and stir in milk.

❖ Cook, stirring constantly, until
mixture thickens slightly. Add salt,
pepper and cheese.

❖ Cook and stir until cheese melts.
Slowly add hot mixture to egg yolks

❖ Serve immediately with the rice.
Makes 6 servings.

Chicken Gumbo Soup

1 onion, finely chopped
1/2 cup chopped green pepper
1 rib celery, diced
4 tablespoons margarine
1/2 pound boneless chicken, cut into
1/2-inch cubes
1/4 pound fresh okra, or
1 10 1/2-ounce package frozen okra
3/4 cup stewed tomatoes
1/4 cup uncooked rice
1 46-ounce can chicken broth
White pepper
Old Bay Seasoning

❖ Sauté onion, green pepper and
celery in 2 tablespoons margarine
in skillet until onion is golden.
Remove and set aside. Add remaining 2 tablespoons margarine and
sauté chicken cubes until lightly
browned. Stir in okra which has
been cut into thin slices. Stir occasionally. Combine all ingredients in
a heavy pot. Add half a chicken
broth can of water. Simmer on low
for 20 to 30 minutes or until chick-
en, vegetables and rice are thoroughly cooked. Add about 1/8 to 1/4
teaspoon Old Bay Seasoning, as
desired. Cook 10 minutes longer.

Cream of Chicken Soup with Egg and Lemon Sauce

1 stick butter
2 cups onions, finely chopped
3 cloves garlic, finely chopped
4 quarts chicken stock
1 head escarole
2 tablespoons chicken base or
8 chicken cubes
1½ cups milk
1½ cups flour
3 egg yolks
½ cup light cream
Juice of 2 lemons
¼ cup chopped chives or thinly
sliced scallions
¼ cup chopped fresh parsley
½ cup minced dehydrated onions
Salt and pepper to taste
½ teaspoon cayenne pepper

❖ Place butter, onions and garlic in a heavy stockpot and sauté onions and garlic until they are soft and transparent about 3 to 5 minutes. In a separate pot, boil chicken stock. Add clean head of escarole. Cover and boil for 10 minutes. Strain and combine chicken stock with onion and garlic mixture. (Escarole may be used for sautéing as a separate side dish.) Bring to a rapid boil. Add chicken base or chicken cubes, then add thickening agent (milk and flour that has been blended). Reduce heat, stir and cook out flour taste for 5 to 8 minutes. Do not scorch. In a bowl, combine egg yolks, cream and lemon juice, beat. Add 1 quart of hot creamed chicken soup, a cup at a time to the beaten egg yolk mixture. Whisk each cup into egg mixture until the entire quart has been used. Transfer this mixture to main stockpot and whisk well. Remove from heat. Add chopped chives or sliced scallions, chopped parsley and minced dehydrated onions. Add salt and pepper to taste and cayenne pepper. Reheat soup in a double boiler.

from the Kitchen of
F.E. LaMontagne, D.M.D.
Pascoag Gastronomic Society

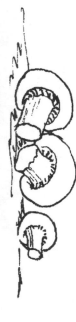

Cream of Mushroom Soup à la Higgins

This is called à la Higgins because that is who came to lunch the day I made up this recipe.

½ pound mushrooms, thinly sliced
6 tablespoons butter
2 tablespoons flour
1 16-ounce can chicken broth
1 cup half and half
White pepper

❖ Sauté sliced mushrooms in 3 tablespoons butter and set aside. In a saucepan, make a roux using remaining 3 tablespoons butter and 2 tablespoons flour, cooking together for 3 to 4 minutes or until mixture is slightly browned. Add chicken broth and half and half stirring constantly until thickened. Add sautéed mushrooms and a few shakes of white pepper and salt to taste. Stir continuously. Serve hot. Serves 3 to 4 for a soup course.

Mushroom Beef Barley Soup

As with most soups, it is much better the next day.

1 tablespoon margarine
1/2 pound ground round or very lean ground sirloin
1 medium onion, finely chopped
1/2 pound fresh mushrooms, finely chopped
2 13 1/2-ounce cans beef broth
1 beef broth can water
1/2 cup uncooked quick barley
Salt and pepper to taste

❖ In a heavy soup pot, melt margarine, then sauté ground round, onion and mushrooms for about 4 to 5 minutes.

❖ Add beef broth and water and simmer, covered, for 15 to 20 minutes.

❖ Add 1/2 cup quick cooking barley and cook for another 12 to 15 minutes. Season with salt and pepper to taste.

❖ When cooked, pour mixture into an blender and blend just enough to break down barley kernels and thicken mixture. Serve hot or may be frozen.

Sara's Onion Soup

First made with Auntie B at age 3

8 large sweet onions, thinly sliced
3 tablespoons margarine
1 48-ounce can chicken broth
1/2 can water
4 beef bouillon cubes
Salt and pepper to taste
Toasted slices of French or Italian bread
Fresh grated cheese such as Cheddar, Colby, Swiss, mozzarella or Parmesan or a combination

❖ In a large skillet or soup pot, sauté onion in margarine until golden brown. Do not burn. Add broth, water and beef cubes, stirring often. Simmer entire mixture for 20 to 25 minutes. Season to taste. May be refrigerated or frozen at this point. To serve, put hot soup in ovenproof crock—1 large or individual. Heat oven to 400° F. Put filled soup cups on a cookie sheet. Top soup with toasted slices of French or Italian bread. Sprinkle with fresh grated cheese. We like a combination. Heat 5 to 10 minutes or until cheese is bubbly and slightly brown.

❖ Note: If onions are not very sweet, add a little sugar while simmering. Use Vidalia onions when in season.

Potato and Leek Soup

3 leeks
3 tablespoons butter
3 ribs celery, diced
5 large potatoes
3 cups chicken broth
1 peeled carrot
3 cups whole milk or 1 can skim milk and 1 can water
Salt and pepper to taste

❖ Clean leeks well with cold water. Trim roots and dark green thick tops. Cut lengthwise from top almost through white. Separate carefully and rinse well. Cut into thin slices. Melt butter in pot and sauté leeks and celery for about 10 minutes, stirring often. Do not brown. Add 1 1/2 cups water. Cook, covered, for 10 minutes more. Add diced potatoes, 3 cups chicken broth and carrot, cook for 10 to 15 minutes more, then add 3 cups milk, salt and pepper to taste. Cook, covered, for 10 minutes more or until potatoes are tender.

Wednesday's Soup

Serve with crusty rolls. Even better reheated and served the next day.

1 large onion, minced
3 tablespoons margarine
6 large potatoes, diced
1 16-ounce can chicken broth or
1 bouillon cube and 2 cups water
1 16-ounce can creamed corn
2 16-ounce cans water
1/4 to 1/2 pound shelled fresh shrimp
  or 1 6-ounce can shrimp
1 12-ounce can skim evaporated milk
Salt and pepper to taste

❖ Sauté minced onion in margarine in a large heavy saucepan. When onion is soft and translucent, add potatoes, chicken broth, corn and water.

❖ Simmer, covered, for 1/2 to 3/4 hour or until potatoes are cooked. Add peeled shrimp or canned shrimp. Cook for 5 minutes. Add evaporated milk. Heat thoroughly.

The Rural School Lunch

"The hot lunch has proven successful," according to an Extension Bulletin, one of the earliest, from the Rhode Island State College Extension Service dated Kingston, Rhode Island, January, 1919. One of the authors, believe it or not, was still going strong during the 50s. I did a 4-H canning demonstration with her at Knight's Farm. Who was this ambitious woman? None other than Annie S. Hoxsie. Unfortunately, the school lunch picture has changed in Rhode Island as well as nationwide. Maybe we should look back in history and take a lesson from the fare which was served back then. Soups were very popular, and here's one to try!

1919 Cream of Tomato Soup

2 quarts milk
1 cup flour
1 tablespoon salt
Dash of pepper
4 tablespoons butter or margarine
2 quarts tomatoes
1 onion, sliced

❖ Heat milk in double boiler reserving 1 cup. Mix flour with the cold milk rubbing out all lumps. Add this slowly to hot milk, stirring until thickened, then add seasonings and butter. Long cooking will improve flavor and will not thicken the sauce more. Cook the tomato with the onion, put through strainer and just before ready to serve, combine with the milk mixture and serve immediately. Serves 15.

❖ Note: Cream of vegetable soups are made by adding pulp of a cooked vegetable to thin white sauce.

Venus De Milo Soup

A quick and easy soup which serves a multitude. This famous first course at a popular local restaurant in Swansea, Massachusetts, has won many prizes locally in food competition.

1 pound ground beef
1 46-ounce can chicken broth
1 16-ounce can chicken broth
1 quart water
1 1-ounce package dry onion soup mix
2 ribs celery, finely diced
1 16-ounce can stewed tomatoes
1 10½-ounce package frozen mixed vegetables
1 cup orzo or ditalini pasta
1 tablespoon Worcestershire sauce

❖ In a large pot, brown ground beef and drain any fat. Add chicken broth, water, onion soup mix and celery. Boil for 20 minutes, add stewed tomatoes which have been crushed and mixed vegetables. Simmer for 15 to 20 minutes. Add pasta and Worcestershire sauce and boil for 10 to 12 minutes. Serves 10 to 12.

Hunter Stew

Years ago, about 20 or so, a very delightful luncheon place operated in downtown Providence call Julienne's. One of the pleasures of the choice of recipes was how simple they were. Actually this is not Julienne's recipe. Her method of scrubbing and not peeling her vegetables made for easy preparation and a different texture, which nowadays is called fiber. This really is Hunt-her Stew. Her (is me) using what I hunted for in my refrigerator and freezer and that's where the name for this recipe originated.

Hunt-Her Stew

May be served immediately but is even better the next day. If you're not a beer drinker, the flavor won't be the same...but you may substitute water and beef bouillon cubes instead.

1 to 1½ pounds stew beef
Flour
Salt and pepper
1 large onion, finely chopped
2 ribs celery, finely chopped
¼ pound fresh mushrooms, sliced
3 carrots, sliced in rounds
5 medium new potatoes, red or white
1 cup fresh or frozen cut green beans
1 12-ounce can beer
1 tomato, chopped, optional

❖ Dredge 1-inch cubes of beef in flour, pepper and salt. brown in a little fat in the bottom of soup kettle. Add onion and celery. Cook for about 20 minutes. Add remaining ingredients. Mix lightly. Add enough water to cover entire mixture. Cover tightly and cook about 20 to 25 minutes or until vegetables are cooked. Check potatoes for doneness, should be fairly soft. Don't worry about other vegetables; they'll be done just right.

Jane's Oven Beef Stew

1 to 1½ pounds stew beef or round
1 10½-ounce can beef bouillon
1 soup can red wine
1 soup can water
1 large onion, diced
½ green pepper, sliced
1 clove garlic
4 white potatoes, cut up
4 carrots, cut up
1 small white turnip, cut up
2 parsnips, diced
1 cup frozen green beans
1 cup fresh mushrooms
1 cup frozen green peas
Salt and pepper to taste
Worcestershire sauce to taste

❖ Brown beef in a Dutch oven. Add bouillon, wine and half the water; simmer at 325° F for 2 hours. Add onion, pepper, garlic and remaining water. Continue to cook for another ½ hour. Add potatoes, carrots, turnip and parsnips. Cook for another ¾ hour. Add beans, mushrooms and frozen peas. Season with salt, pepper and Worcestershire sauce. Cook about another 15 minutes or until mushrooms are done. A great one-dish meal.

Bob's Bouillabaisse

Bob says the recipe can be varied depending on ingredients available and what the "cook likes"; just substitute another kind of seafood so you will be able to serve this number of servings. You can also divide recipe in half,... better still, if there's anything left, it freezes well. Reheat in microwave.

½ cup olive oil
6 ounces fresh mushrooms, sliced
1 large onion, finely chopped
2 large cloves garlic, mashed
1 green pepper, finely chopped
3 tablespoons chopped parsley
1 28-ounce can whole tomatoes
2 bay leaves
⅛ teaspoon cayenne pepper
1½ cups dry white or red wine
¾ to 1 pound white fish, scrod, cod, pollock, hake or other white fish into chunks
½ pound cooked lobster meat, cut into chunks
½ to ¾ pound shrimp, peeled and deveined, any size but colossal
½ pint oysters and juice
½ pound scallops, sea or bay
1 pint little necks or cherrystones, in shell
3 king crab legs, in shell

❖ Heat oil in a large heavy pan. Add mushrooms, onion, garlic, green pepper and parsley. Sauté for about 10 minutes, stirring occasionally. Add tomatoes and juice, bay leaves, pepper and wine; simmer for 1½ hours on low. Add fish and cook, covered, for 15 to 20 minutes. Add lobster meat, shrimp, oysters, scallops, little necks that have been well scrubbed and left in shells and crab legs. When little necks open, bouillabaisse is done. When done, serve in chowder plates, being sure to give everyone something of everything; ladle broth over seafood. Serves 8 to 10.

❖ Note: Great served with a very crusty bread, Caesar or spinach salad and, of course, a wine. A fruit dessert is a nice accompaniment.

Chowders

The ingredients are milk, a fatty substance, which is usually salt pork, potatoes, or crackers, often both, and in addition to these, one of the following: fish, which may be either fresh or salt; green corn, fresh or canned; quahogs or clams. A chowder consisting mainly of milk, potatoes and crackers and flavored with a little salt codfish is perhaps the most economical of these dishes.

Little Compton Mussel Chowder

1/4 pound salt pork, diced
1 cup slivered onions
2 cups tomatoes, fresh or canned
1 cup green peppers, thinly sliced
2 cups white potatoes, diced
2 cups corn, fresh or canned
1 peck mussels
Salt to taste
Black pepper
Cayenne red pepper
Paprika

❖ Fry salt pork and slivered onions in a heavy saucepot until light brown.

Do not remove pork. Add tomatoes and peppers; simmer on low for 2 hours. Add potatoes and corn; cook until tender. Wash mussels in the shells and put in a big pot and steam, covered. As the shells, open take out mussels, removing any stones or seaweed that may be attached and put mussels in a bowl. Strain the mussel broth into the vegetable mixture. The broth is very salty, so add salt carefully "to taste." Add black pepper, cayenne red pepper and paprika. Put mussels in just before serving.

Chepachet Chowder

A Chepachet landmark, Gautreau's has been in business for years and years—a true family operation. Carl and I had our wedding reception here, and our choice for appetizer was Quahog Chowder. George gave me this recipe many years ago, but I still prefer to go there and let the family make the chowder. Here is my adaptation for a small chowder.

4 to 5 quarts quahogs, in shell
5 pounds potatoes
3 large onions
3 ounces salt pork
(Salt—omit or to taste)
1 teaspoon pepper
1/2 teaspoon Accent
Water and milk

❖ Wash quahogs and put in large kettle. Put in water to just below the shells. Steam open. Remove entire quahog from shell and put through meat grinder. Save the broth and strain through cheesecloth. Peel and dice potatoes and put in cold water. Peel onions and mince through grinder and sauté in fried out salt pork. Remove salt pork before adding onions. Cook until onions are transparent. Add peeled, diced potatoes, salt, pepper and Accent. Add strained broth and enough water to cover potatoes. Cook about 20 minutes or until potatoes are done (soft, but still firm). Add ground quahogs. Should be made at least the day before needed and refrigerated. Add milk to taste and heat very hot. Serve with oyster crackers or pilot crackers.

Ridgeview Farm

The very first time I visited Ridgeview Farm was at a country auction early in the 50s with my parents who had been busy combing the countryside for buys at local auctions. (Remember yard sales and flea markets had not been invented under those names at that time.)

It had a wonderful apple orchard. Well, 20 years later I attended the first of many good times at Ridgeview with the new owners...and the apple orchard had a new function... one of the largest and best Chowder Parties held yearly by Papa John and Jane (otherwise known to many of you as Lieutenant Governor and Mrs. Giovanni Folcarelli). John was one of the best seafood cooks I have known and believe it or not John was not a seafood lover... but he loved to cook.

His recipe for Steamers (see page 98) is one of the best.

Bud's Ridgeview Farm Chowder

"The Chowdermaster was Bud Robinson of Hope, who made this chowder for many years at Democratic outings at Ridgeview Farm."

3/4 pound salt pork
4 pounds onions, chopped
15 pounds potatoes, diced
Juice from quahogs
1 16-ounce can tomato purée
1/2 gallon quahogs, chopped
Salt
Pepper
Basil

❖ Fry salt pork and reserve fat. Brown onions in fat, but do not burn. Add potatoes, quahog juice and enough water to cover the potatoes. Boil until potatoes are soft. Add purée until potatoes are soft. Add purée to desired color. Finally add chopped quahogs and lower heat. Season to taste with salt, pepper and a pinch of basil. Cook over low heat for approximately 1/2 hour. Serve with clam cakes, oyster crackers and of course ice cold watermelon. Serves 25 to 30 generously.

Island Quahog Chowder

1/4 pound salt pork, cut into small cubes
2 medium onions, minced
4 large potatoes, peeled, cubed
2 cups chopped quahogs
1 quart milk
2 cups light cream or half and half
3 tablespoons butter
3 tablespoons flour
Salt and pepper

❖ Sauté salt pork in pan until brown. Remove pork. Sauté onions in pan drippings until lightly brown. Do not burn. Add cubed potatoes and cover with water. Cook for about 15 minutes or until potatoes are cooked. Remove dark stomachs from quahogs before chopping in grinder or food processor. Add juice and quahogs to cooked potato mixture. Heat milk, cream and butter together in another pan until mixture is scalded. Do not boil. Add to quahog mixture. Stir flour into a little cold milk to dissolve and slowly stir into heated mixture. Add salt and pepper to taste. Cook slowly for 8 to 10 minutes. Serve hot with pilot or oyster crackers.

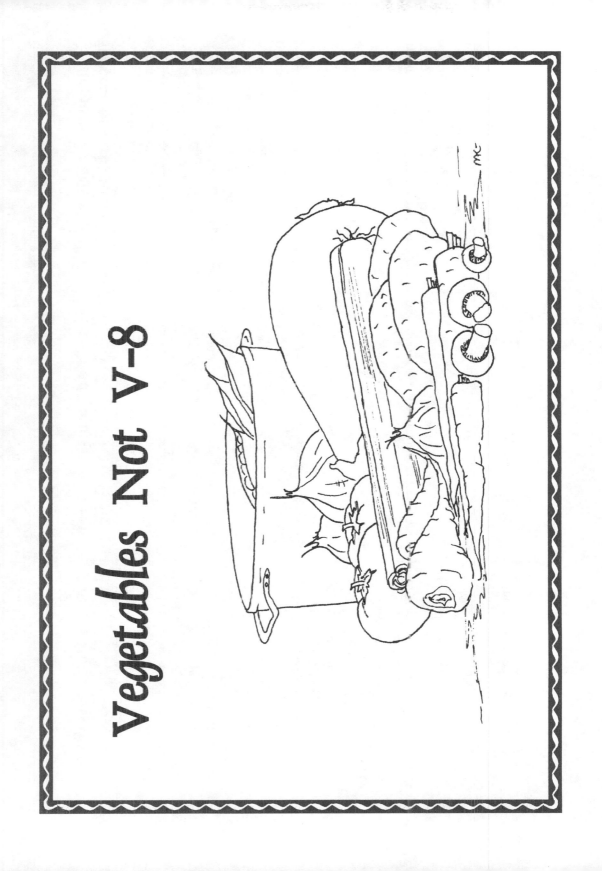

Vegetables Not V-8

Grandmother Zarli's Stuffed Artichokes or Peppers

4 large artichokes or peppers
1/4 cup olive oil
1 teaspoon chopped garlic
1/4 cup Parmesan cheese
2 anchovies, mashed
1/4 cup fresh coarse bread crumbs
2 tablespoons chopped parsley
1/2 teaspoon salt
1/2 teaspoon pepper
1/2 cup raisins
1 cup black olives
1 cup chicken broth

❖ Wash and trim artichokes or peppers.

❖ Mix 2 tablespoons olive oil with remaining ingredients. Divide mixture into 4 portions and fill artichokes or peppers. Place in saucepan with 1 cup chicken broth. Drizzle remaining olive oil over vegetables. Cover and simmer for 30 to 40 minutes.

Sweet and Sour Green Beans

A welcome change from the usual green bean casserole

1 pound fresh green beans
4 slices bacon
2 tablespoons finely chopped onion, optional
1 tablespoon vinegar
1/4 teaspoon sugar
Salt and pepper to taste

❖ Cook beans until just tender. Drain. While beans are cooking, fry bacon until crisp. Drain on paper towels. Add onion to bacon drippings and cook until tender (not brown) over low heat. Stir in vinegar, sugar, salt, pepper and finely crumbled bacon. Pour over hot beans. If bacon is very fat, pour off some of the drippings before cooking onion.

❖ Note: Should be served warm; can be reheated in microwave.

Carrots in Orange Sauce

2 1/2 pounds carrots
1 cup orange juice
1/2 cup sugar
3 tablespoons flour
1 tablespoon grated orange rind
1/2 teaspoon salt
2 tablespoons butter or margarine

❖ Peel carrots, slice as desired, and cook until tender, about 15 minutes or in your microwave. For the sauce combine orange juice, sugar, flour, grated orange rind, salt and butter and cook stirring constantly for 5 minutes. When done mix with cooked carrots and serve immediately. Can be made beforehand and reheated successfully in the microwave. Serves 10 to 12.

Carrot Marmalade

2 1/2 cups ground carrots
3 1/2 cups sugar
2 lemons, ground

❖ Mix ingredients together in a heavy saucepan. Boil about 20 minutes or until thickened. Put in sterilized jars. Seal. Makes 4 half pints.

Citrus Carrot Marmalade

4 cups (2 pounds) carrots, cooked
   until tender then ground
2 oranges, grated rind and pulp
2 lemons, grated rind and juice
2³/4 pounds of sugar
¹/2 bottle of Certo

❖ Mix all except Certo together in
heavy pot and bring to rolling boil,
stirring constantly. Boil for 5
minutes. Remove from fire, stir in
Certo, and pour quickly into hot
sterile glasses. Cover with a thin
layer of melted paraffin and allow
to cool. Store in a cool dry place.
Makes about 9 (6-ounce) glasses.

Prudence Island

Marie's Stuffed Eggplant

1 eggplant, about 2 to 3 pounds
1 teaspoon parsley
1 green pepper
Salt and pepper
1 teaspoon oregano
2 tablespoons butter
Olive oil
2 cloves garlic, chopped
1 8-ounce can tomato sauce

❖ Cut off top of eggplant and scoop
out center. Cut pulp in small pieces.
Add parsley, diced green pepper,
salt, pepper, oregano and butter.

❖ Restuff. Put a skewer through the
top to hold in place.

❖ Heat olive oil in a saucepan and fry
out the garlic being carefully not to
burn. Put eggplant in pan and cook
on all sides until a little crinkly look-
ing, then add 1 cup tomato sauce.
Cover and simmer for 20 to 30
minutes, till soft when pierced.

Stuffed Eggplant Soufflé

1 eggplant, about 2 pounds
2 cloves garlic, minced
1 medium onion, chopped
1 cup chopped mushrooms, about 6
   ounces fresh
1 tablespoon oil
2 egg yolks, beaten
¹/2 cup dry bread crumbs
¹/2 cup grated Parmesan cheese
¹/2 cup chopped walnuts
¹/2 teaspoon nutmeg
¹/4 teaspoon salt
¹/4 teaspoon pepper
2 egg whites

❖ Cut eggplant in half lengthwise and
remove stem. Scoop out inside leaving a fairly thick shell. Cut inside
pieces into 1-inch cubes and cook
with ¹/2 cup water in a covered
microwave dish on High for about 8
to 10 minutes or until soft.

❖ Chop garlic, onion, and mushrooms, sauté lightly in oil. Add egg
yolks, bread crumbs, cheese and
nuts to pulp; add nutmeg, salt and
pepper. Beat egg whites until stiff
but not dry. Fold them into other
ingredients lightly. Spoon mixture
into eggplant halves. Place them
in a pan with a little water and
bake at 325° F for 30 minutes or
until puffy and top
is lightly browned.
Serves 4.

Eggplant Casserole

2 eggplant, peeled and sliced
2 pound ground beef
2 12-ounce packages low-fat skim
   mozzarella cheese
2 cups low-fat cottage cheese

❖ Dip the eggplant in flour. Fry them
in a small amount of oil and drain
on paper towels. Brown the beef in
a skillet; pour off any excess oil. In
a 9-inch square pan, layer 1/3 meat,
1/3 eggplant, 1/3 mozzarella cheese,
and 1/3 cottage cheese. Repeat layers.
Bake at 300° F for 1 to 1 1/2 hours.

Barbara's Vidalia Onions

4 large peeled Vidalia onions or other
   sweet onions
1/4 pound margarine
3/4 cup water
3/4 cup stuffing mix

❖ Cut onions into wedges; put in
bottom of 2 quart casserole. Cut up
margarine and put over top, add
water and sprinkle with stuffing
mix. Cover. Bake at 375° F for about
20 to 30 minutes.

Lyonnaise Potatoes

12 medium red potatoes
2 medium red onions, diced
Fresh rosemary
1 12-ounce can chicken broth
1 12-ounce can beef broth
Fresh ground black pepper
1 stick margarine or butter

❖ Scrub potatoes and slice partially
through, like a fan. In a deep baking
dish, put potatoes on top of diced
onions. Sprinkle sprigs of fresh rosemary over mixture. Pack potatoes
tightly into pan. Add broth to
potatoes. Sprinkle with black pepper
and margarine. Bake, uncovered, at
400° F for 35 to 40 minutes or until
potatoes are soft and golden brown.

Shirley's Quick and Easy Potatoes

*This is a great buffet dish and can be
made the day before. Not an original by
any means, but a recipe shared with me
by neighbor, best friend and my doubles
partner. We've fooled many with this
timesaver, enough so many say they
would buy this book because of it!*

1 32-ounce package frozen hashed
   brown potatoes
1 pint sour cream
1 10 1/2-ounce can cream of chicken
   soup
1 4-ounce package frozen chopped
   onion
1/2 cup margarine, melted
10 ounces Cheddar cheese, shredded
   Crushed cornflakes

❖ Mix first 6 ingredients thoroughly,
bake in a buttered 9x13-inch baking
dish. Top mixture with crushed
cornflakes. Bake at 350° F for 1 to
1 1/2 hours. I like it cooked for almost 2 hours, since I like the
potatoes mealy, but many of my
guests like them a little crunchy.

❖ Note: For a slight change, use
another 1/2 package of potatoes.
Add 1 cup skim milk and use non-
fat sour cream, 1/3 less salt soup,
omit the margarine and use skim
mozzarella shredded cheese for
less calories and fat. Use a 3-quart
casserole.

Dottie's Squash Flowers

A favorite of those who have a garden; if you don't, many large supermarkets or natural food stores sell them. Rhode Islanders eat as is and on the Vineyard they "dust with cinnamon or nutmeg."

2 to 3 dozen squash flowers

Light Batter:
1 cup flour
1/2 cup milk
1/2 cup cold water
2 tablespoons oil
1 teaspoon baking powder
1/2 teaspoon salt
1 egg, well beaten

❖ When picking buds, avoid those that show tiny squash. Best picked early or late in the day. Remove stem, open flour and wash well under cold water, removing stamen and pistil from each blossom. Flatten and pat dry with paper towel. Beat together flour, milk, water, oil, baking powder, salt and egg to make a thin batter. Dip flowers into flour, then dip individually into batter with tongs allowing excess batter to drip in bowl. Fry in 1 to 1½ inches hot vegetable oil until golden brown. Drain on paper towels. Serve as a side dish.

❖ Note: Light batter can also be used for shrimp and clams.

Florence's Zucchini Squash Casserole

This recipe was given to me by a teacher I had in the third grade, many, many years later, with the following note attached which was much appreciated. "To friend Barbara, a noted excellent cook, Florence E. Logee..."

2 pounds zucchini, shredded
2 medium onions, finely chopped
1/4 teaspoon salt
4 slices bread, crumbled
1 egg, slightly beaten
1 tablespoon margarine
Shredded sharp cheese

❖ Combine all ingredients, except cheese and put in a buttered 1½-quart baking dish. Bake at 350° F for 50 to 60 minutes. In the last 15 minutes, taste and top with cheese.

O'Shea's Zucchini and Corn

This recipe was passed on by an Aquidneck Island friend who has served it with rave reviews from her family.

8 slices bacon
4 medium zucchini, sliced
1 16-ounce can whole kernel corn
1 4-ounce can green chilies
1 to 1½ cups shredded Cheddar cheese

❖ Fry bacon until crisp, crumble and set aside. In 3 tablespoons of bacon fat, add zucchini and corn with liquid. Simmer, uncovered, until zucchini is tender and liquid has evaporated.

❖ Add chilies which have been seasoned to taste with Tabasco and garlic powder.

❖ Add cheese and simmer long enough for cheese to melt. Serve immediately.

❖ Note: Use Longhorn, Cheddar, Monterey Jack or a combination of cheeses.

Succotash

Much has been mentioned in history about a dish called "succotash" which early settlers learned to make from the Indians. The how's and why's of this dish are apparent, but a definitive documentation of what variety of bean used is unclear. Depending on the source, the recipe does not really give a clue. Many feel that a form of the lima bean was used, while others range from red kidney to shell beans (horticulture beans), which are red and white before cooking and then become a small brown bean when cooked.

Some sources indicate beans were cooked fresh with salt pork and mixed with "green corn." Others contend dried beans (all types) and dried corn were used, which for very early days makes sense. All in all, here's a recipe for "corn and beans" or "Island Succotash" which can be served as a main dish or as a side dish.

Island Succotash

2 pounds shell (horticulture) beans or
2 16-ounce cans shell beans
Water
¼ pound lean salt pork or
4 slices bacon
6 ears corn, steamed 3 minutes or
1 16-ounce can whole kernel corn
Salt and pepper

❖ Shell beans, rinse and put in sauce-pan with bacon or salt pork. Cover with water.

❖ Simmer, covered, for 20 to 30 minutes or until beans soften. Do not drain.

❖ Add corn which has been cut off the cob, or canned corn. Mix.

❖ Serve with butter, salt and pepper at the table.

❖ Note: This mixture freezes well and may be reheated in microwave.

Utility Company Home Service Departments

Utility companies Home Service Departments were popular during the 30s through the 70s. Some of you may remember "The Girl in White" Marie O'Brien, of the Providence Gas Company; Mary Reis of Newport Gas and Electric; Betty Bradford (Anne Zeigler) of the Narragansett Electric; Jerry Foley of Blackstone Gas and Electric; as well as countless others. A former 4-H member Trudy Duffy Willis was also a home service home economist during that time. The home economist acted as a consumer specialist to owners of new appliances providing product information, cooking schools, club programs, special presentations for Holiday cooking and special diets, and, last but not least, a person to call to help solve your "cooking problems," a real community service available to all.

Two delightful vegetable recipes from the 30s are as popular now as then.

Scalloped Sweet Potatoes and Pineapple

6 medium sweet potatoes
6 slices pineapple, cut into small pieces
3/4 cup pineapple juice
1/2 cup packed brown sugar
1/4 cup water
3 tablespoons margarine

❖ Peel and slice sweet potatoes into 1/4-inch slices. Arrange alternate layers of sweet potatoes and pineapple in a 1 1/2-quart casserole, 4 layers in all. Combine the pineapple juice, brown sugar, water and margarine. Boil for 3 minutes; pour over casserole. Cover. Bake at 350° F for 1 hour. Serves 6.

Narragansett Electric

Crunchy Fried Tomatoes

4 firm ripe or green medium tomatoes (about 1 1/2 pounds)
1 egg, beaten
1 cup dry bread crumbs
1/3 cup margarine
Salt and pepper

❖ Wash tomatoes; cut into 3/4-inch slices. If desired, peel tomatoes before cutting. Dip slices into egg and then into crumbs. Melt margarine in large skillet; add tomato slices; cook, turning once until golden brown. Season to taste. Serves 4.

Providence Gas Company

Turnip Casserole

1 medium-sized turnip, cooked and mashed
1 large egg, beaten
1/4 cup cream of wheat
3 tablespoons melted butter
1 teaspoon salt
Dash of pepper
1 tablespoon sugar
Margarine

❖ To prepared turnip add egg, cream of wheat, melted butter, salt, pepper, and sugar and stir ingredients until thoroughly mixed. Grease a 2-quart casserole with margarine and fill with turnip mixture. Bake, uncovered, at 375° F for 30 minutes. Serve hot.

❖ Note: Use white or yellow turnip.

Louise's Vegetable Platter

For 1, 2 or 10...In a large saucepan, put prepared vegetables "right from the farm," whether it be Bartlett's, Blanchard's, or ....

New potatoes
Carrots
Onions
Cauliflower
Green and yellow beans

❖ There is nothing to match fresh vegetables cooked until just barely done, about 20 minutes, and served steaming hot with butter, pepper and salt.

❖ Even if you're not a vegetarian, you'll come back for more.

Tom's Vegetarian Dish

Roots, Herbs and Berries according to Mike. So says his mother about this vegetarian dish made especially for his brother Tom, who is really watching HIS Diet... I was asked to taste it for my approval and I replied, "Not bad!"

1　16-ounce can black, turtle or black-eyed beans
1　16-ounce can garbanzo beans (chick-peas)
1　10-ounce can corn niblets
1　16-ounce can corn niblets
2　cups corn
2　16-ounce can stewed Italian plum tomatoes
2　tablespoons salsa, hot or mild
　　Chopped cilantro, optional

❖ Put all ingredients, except for cilantro in a 2-quart casserole.

❖ Heat thoroughly in microwave. Top with cilantro before serving.

❖ Can be served hot or at room temperature, with some very crusty bread.

❖ Note: Don't drain vegetables.

Vegetables Olé

1/2　pound fresh green beans
2　slices bacon
2　tablespoons chopped onion
1　teaspoon flour
3 to 4　tomatoes, peeled and sliced
2　cups corn
2　tablespoons chopped green pepper
1　teaspoon sugar
3/4　teaspoon salt
　　Dash of pepper

❖ Cook green beans until tender (or use leftovers).

❖ Sauté bacon and onion. Blend flour into bacon fat. Add bean liquid (1/2 cup). Add beans, other vegetables, sugar, salt and pepper.

❖ Simmer, covered, for 7 minutes or until corn is tender. Serves 4 to 6.

Wild Rice with Nuts

This is the kind of recipe you can change the amounts and ingredients to your own taste.

1　cup uncooked wild rice (1/2 pound)
5 1/2　cups chicken or beef broth
3/4　cup coarsely chopped pecans
1　cup golden raisins
　　Grated rind of 1 large orange
1/4　cup chopped fresh mint
3 to 4　scallions, chopped
1/4　cup olive oil
1/3　cup orange juice
1　teaspoon salt
　　Freshly ground black pepper

❖ Rinse rice in cold water. Put in a deep saucepan with stock and gently simmer, uncovered, for about 45 minutes or until most of liquid is absorbed. Drain. Add remaining ingredients. Let stand at least 2 hours or more for best flavors. Serve at room temperature. Serves 6.

Marinated Carrot Salad

I was very surprised when editing a cookbook for the local historical society that 10 recipes for marinated carrots had been submitted for testing and consideration...well, here's number 11...hope you'll like it as much as I did.

3 pounds carrots
1 green pepper
1 large red onion
1 cup salad oil
1 cup sugar
2/3 cup cider vinegar
1 teaspoon dry mustard
1/2 teaspoon dillweed
1 teaspoon prepared mustard
1/2 teaspoon garlic salt
1 10 1/2-ounce can undiluted tomato soup

❖ Peel and slice carrots diagonally and cook for 5 to 8 minutes, not mushy. Drain. In a large bowl, put carrots and thinly sliced pepper and onion. Mix together salad oil, sugar, vinegar and remainder of ingredients. Pour over carrots. Marinate and chill for several hours before serving. This will stay fresh for at least 3 weeks if it lasts that long.

Corn Relish

12 ears sweet corn
1 medium head cabbage, chopped
4 green and red peppers, chopped
1 cup granulated sugar
2 tablespoons mustard
1 1/2 tablespoons salt
3 cups vinegar

❖ Cut corn off cob. Blend all ingredients together and boil for 20 minutes, put in sterilized jars; seal.

❖ Note: Always use preserving jars.

German Potato Salad

Several slices bacon, fried crisp
6 large potatoes (cold boiled), diced
1 onion, finely sliced

❖ To the bacon fat add 1/2 cup vinegar, 1 tablespoon sugar, 1/4 teaspoon salt and pepper to taste. Pour this mixture over potatoes and onion. Serve hot or cold.

Mother's Camp Coleslaw

This recipe was from an extension friend, who was one of the tourists we relish as our bread and butter in the islands, but the island she visited was the Island of Maui, Hawaii. It's a great new way to make coleslaw, it has all the ingredients of success—basic ingredients, easy to prepare, serves a lot, tastes great and can be made beforehand—great for any mealtime—family or for company.

1 medium head green cabbage, chopped fine or grated
1 medium onion, chopped
1 cup sugar
1 cup cider vinegar
1 teaspoon sugar
1 teaspoon salt
1 teaspoon prepared mustard
1 teaspoon celery seed
1 cup salad oil

❖ Put half of cabbage in bowl; sprinkle with onion, add rest of cabbage and pour 1 cup of sugar over cabbage; set aside. bring vinegar, sugar, salt, mustard and celery seed to a boil; add oil. Remove from heat and pour over cabbage. Do not mix but let cabbage mixture stand for several hours or overnight. Toss prior to serving.

❖ Slaw will keep up to two weeks when mixed.

Spinach Mushroom Salad

Simple but very tasty. From a potluck supper for the NRI Extension Service. "I often make a double batch of dressing as a single batch may not be quite enough," says Linda.

1 pound fresh spinach
1/4 pound fresh mushrooms, sliced
3 hard-boiled eggs, diced
1 bunch scallions, sliced
8 slices bacon, cooked crisp, crumbled
1/2 cup vegetable oil
3 tablespoons vinegar
1 teaspoon sugar
1/4 teaspoon salt
1/4 teaspoon dry mustard
1/8 teaspoon freshly ground black pepper

❖ Remove stems from spinach; wash leaves and pat dry. Tear into bite-sized pieces. Combine spinach, mushrooms, eggs, scallions and bacon in a large bowl.

❖ Combine oil, vinegar, sugar and seasonings in a jar. Cover with lid and shake to blend. Top spinach mixture with dressing just before serving. Yields 6 to 8 good-sized servings.

Vineyard Summer Salad

1/2 pound cooked, shelled shrimp
Cayenne red pepper
1/2 lemon, fresh squeezed
4 red boiled potatoes
2 scallions
1/2 cup green peas
1/2 cup mayonnaise
1/2 green pepper in strips
1/2 cup sliced beets

❖ In a large bowl, put shrimp in bottom and sprinkle with cayenne pepper and lemon juice. Cube red potatoes. Trim and dice scallions, add to bowl with green peas. Mix lightly with mayonnaise and refrigerate for 1 hour or more. When ready to serve, arrange on a bed of red or leafy green lettuce. Garnish with strips of green pepper and sliced beets. If more flavor is desired, serve additional lemon wedges and mayonnaise on the side.

Winter Salad a la Herman

Red and green leafy lettuce
Sliced beets
Seasoned croutons
Cauliflower florets
Sliced red pepper
Caesar-type dressing

❖ Arrange lettuce on individual salad plates, making a bed of greens. Garnish with sliced beets, croutons, cauliflower and red pepper. Sprinkle lightly with Caesar dressing.

Prince Edward Island Mayonnaise

1 cup vinegar
3/4 cup sugar
1 egg (1/4 cup egg substitute)
1/2 teaspoon salt
1 tablespoon dry mustard
1 tablespoon flour
1 cup milk
3 tablespoons margarine

❖ In a saucepan, bring the vinegar to a boil. In a bowl, mix remaining ingredients well. Add to hot vinegar mixture and stir constantly until thickened.

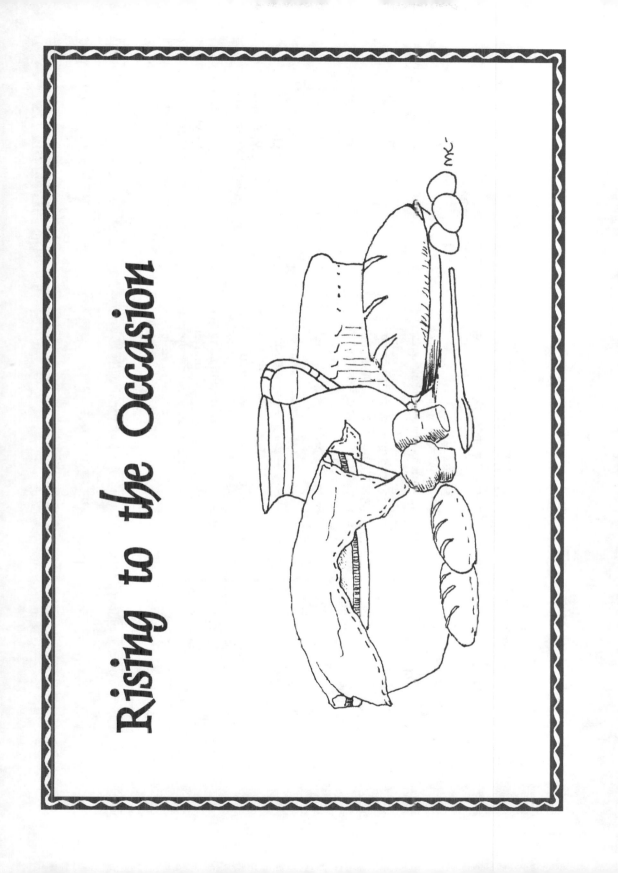

Rising to the Occasion

Baked Brown Bread

1 cup sifted flour
1 teaspoon salt
1/2 cup sugar
2 cups graham flour (whole wheat)
2 teaspoons baking soda
2 cups buttermilk
1/2 cup molasses

❖ Grease ten 6-ounce metal frozen juice cans and use as baking pans.

❖ Sift together flour, salt, sugar and graham flour.

❖ Dissolve baking soda in buttermilk. Combine buttermilk and molasses with flour mixture.

❖ Place 1/3 cup batter in each can. Cover tightly with foil. Place on cookie sheet.

❖ Bake at 350° F for 30 minutes. Let can remain for 5 minutes with foil on after taking from oven. Remove bread from cans.

Carl's Oven Brown Bread

A must with baked beans!

2 cups natural all bran
1 1/2 cups raisins
4 tablespoons shortening
1 cup molasses
1 1/2 cups boiling water
2 eggs
2 cups flour
1 teaspoon salt
2 teaspoons baking soda
1 teaspoon cinnamon

❖ Combine first 5 ingredients; stir until shortening is melted. Beat in 2 eggs. Sift remainder of ingredients and blend with first mixture. Fill well greased 1-pound coffee cans or 1-pound vegetable cans only 2/3 full. Cover tightly with foil and bake at 350° F for about 40 to 50 minutes. Bread will pull away from edges and a straw will come out clean when done. Cool before slicing. Reheat, wrapped in foil, in oven or in plastic wrap in microwave. Freezes well.

❖ Note: For those who don't like raisins, leave them out; cook a little longer if needed.

Irish Bread

5 cups flour
5 teaspoons baking powder
1 teaspoon salt
1 stick butter
1 cup sugar
2 eggs
2 cups buttermilk
2 cups raisins

❖ Mix together flour, baking powder and salt. In another bowl, cream together butter and sugar until light and fluffy. Add eggs one at a time, beating after each addition. Add buttermilk alternately with dry ingredients. Fold in raisins. Bake in a well greased 10-inch tube pan at 350° F in a 10-inch tube pan for about 1 1/4 hours.

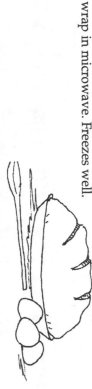

Varnum House

The Varnum House in East Greenwich, RI, was built in 1773 by James Mitchell Varnum, first commander of the Kentish Guards and Brigadier General of the Continental Army. I'm not sure how this recipe originated, but the name Varnum House brings back memories of a wedding reception in the gardens, and in the great parlors of this colonial home, which is now on the National Register for Historic Places. The finger foods which included this delightful lemon bread were enjoyed with champagne and a strolling violinist.

Lemon Tea Bread

1/2 cup soft butter
1 cup sugar
2 eggs, beaten
Grated lemon peel
1½ cups flour
1 teaspoon baking powder
1/2 cup milk

Topping:
1/4 cup sugar
Juice and rind of 1 lemon or 1/2 cup lemon juice

❖ Preheat oven to 375° F. Grease a 9x5-inch loaf pan. Cream together butter and sugar until light. Beat in eggs, then stir in grated lemon peel from 1 lemon. Sift together flour and baking powder, add alternately to egg mixture and milk in the same bowl. Pour into prepared pan, bake about 45 minutes or until light brown. The bread pulls away from edges of pan when done.

❖ Prepare topping by combining sugar, juice and lemon rind. When bread is done, cool for 10 minutes before removing from pan. Remove and poke holes in entire surface. Brush all of juice mixture over top of bread. Do not cut for several hours.

❖ Note: Use only rind of lemon not the white or it will be bitter.

Nantucket Portuguese Bread

3 tablespoons sugar
1 tablespoon salt
2 cups boiling water
3 packages dry yeast
6 to 7 cups flour

❖ Add sugar and salt to boiling water. Mix and let cool. When cool enough, it will be only warm to the touch when put on the inside of your wrist, about 105° F. Add dry yeast and 2 cups flour to water, beating well with mixer. Continue to add flour, a cup at a time. If mixture gets too thick for your mixer, switch to a wooden spoon. When a soft dough is formed, turn out on a floured board. Knead 8 to 10 minutes. Let rise until double in bulk. Punch down. Divide into 3 portions and make 3 round loaves or into 2 portions for large loaves. Place on a greased cookie sheet and let rise until double. Bake 1 hour at 375° F until it sounds hollow when tapped.

From Mrs. "Silver" and her summers cooking in the tea room at Wauwinet in 1928

Portuguese Sweet Bread

2 packages dry yeast
1 1/4 cups sugar
5 1/2 to 6 cups flour
1 1/2 teaspoons salt
1/4 cup water
1 cup milk
1/2 cup margarine
3 eggs, separated

❖ In a large bowl, put yeast, sugar, 2 cups flour and salt, set aside.

❖ Heat water, milk and margarine to 120° F in microwave or in saucepan. If you are not sure of temperature, use a thermometer. Add heated liquid to flour mixture, beat well with mixer for 3 to 4 minutes. Add egg yolks and continue beating 2 to 3 more minutes.

❖ In a small bowl, beat egg whites until stiff, then fold into batter. Add remaining flour a cup at a time, mixing with a wooden spoon or heavy-duty mixer until a soft dough forms. Turn out on a floured board.

❖ Knead 8 to 10 minutes adding flour to the board when needed to prevent sticking. Put a tablespoon

of oil in a clean bowl, put dough in bowl and turn over so all sides are coated with oil. Cover with wax paper and a towel.

❖ Let rise until double in bulk, about 3 to 4 hours. Punch down, divide in half and shape into two round loaves.

❖ Place in greased 8 or 9-inch round pans. Let rise until doubled, about 3 hours. Before baking, brush with milk or milk and egg combination.

❖ Cut a cross on top of each loaf with a sharp knife.

❖ Bake in a slow oven 300° F about 1 to 1 1/2 hours or until golden brown on top and it sounds hollow when tapped. Cool on rack.

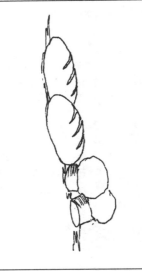

Zucchini Bread

What farm, large or small, doesn't have zucchini? In the islands, it seems that someone always has too many zucchini or too many "blues." This is a recipe which a friend shared with me many years ago....Well, it does help to use up some of "those zucchini."

3 eggs
1 1/2 cups vegetable oil
2 cups shredded zucchini
1 1/2 cups sugar
1 teaspoon vanilla
3 1/4 cups whole wheat flour
2 teaspoons baking soda
3/4 teaspoon salt
3/4 teaspoon ground cloves
3/4 teaspoon allspice
1 teaspoon cinnamon
1/2 cup chopped nuts
1/2 cup raisins
1/4 cup water

❖ Preheat oven to 350° F. Grease and flour loaf pans. In a large bowl, beat eggs, add oil, zucchini, sugar and vanilla, blending well. Sift together dry ingredients, beat slowly into egg mixture, adding nuts, raisins and water until just moistened.

Pour into prepared pans. For large loaves, bake 55 to 60 minutes. For smaller loaves, check at 35 to 40 minutes, bread will pull away from edges of pan when nearly done. For a final check, use a toothpick that should come out clean when inserted in center of bread. Cool for 15 minutes before removing from pan. Do not wrap until bread is completely cool. Freezes well. Can be made in 2 loaf pans 9x5x3 inches or in 4 to 6 smaller or miniature pan.

Block Island Doughnuts

"These doughnuts used to be made in a black cast-iron kettle—suspended from a crane over a fire."

2 eggs
1 cup sugar
1 teaspoon vanilla
1/2 of a nutmeg, grated
2 1/2 cups flour
1 teaspoon baking powder
1/2 teaspoon baking soda
1 cup thick sour milk or buttermilk
3 tablespoons melted shortening
Cinnamon, optional
Confectioners' sugar, optional

❖ Beat eggs until light and fluffy. Add sugar, vanilla and nutmeg. Sift dry ingredients together and add to egg mixture alternately with sour milk and melted shortening. (Add a little more flour, only if needed to keep dough from sticking to board. Dough should be as soft as possible.) Roll out, cut and drop into hot fat. Turn as soon as they rise to top; turn again to brown on both sides. Drain; shake, if desired, in bag with mixture of cinnamon and confectioners' sugar.

Taken from "Taste of Glocester"

Billy's Griddle Cakes

An old Block Island recipe

1 egg
3/4 cup milk
3 tablespoons shortening
1 1/2 cups flour
3 1/2 teaspoons baking powder
3 tablespoons sugar
3/4 teaspoon salt

❖ Beat egg; add milk and shortening. Sift dry ingredients together and add to liquids. Add more milk if thinner cake is desired. Cook on hot griddle; serve at once with any desired topping. Makes about 1 dozen griddle cakes.

Taken from "Taste of Glocester"

Special Apple Muffins

1 cup flour
1 tablespoon baking powder
1/4 teaspoon salt
1 cup rolled oats
1 cup chopped apples
1/4 cup brown sugar
1 egg, beaten
2 tablespoons oil
1/2 cup milk
1/2 cup raisins

Topping:
3 tablespoons brown sugar mixed with 1/2 teaspoon cinnamon

❖ Sift together flour, baking powder and salt. Stir in oats, apples, and brown sugar. In a small bowl mix egg, oil and milk, then add to dry mixture, stirring only until moist. Add raisins. Fill greased muffin tins 2/3 full. Sprinkle with topping and bake at 400° F for 15 to 18 minutes. Remove from pan immediately.

Barbara's Banana Muffins

1 egg
1 cup milk
1/4 cup salad oil
2 cups flour
3 teaspoons baking powder
1/4 teaspoon salt
1/2 cup sugar
1 ripe banana
1/2 cup nuts, chopped, optional
1 teaspoon cinnamon
1/2 cup sugar

❖ Preheat oven to 425° F. Grease or spray 12 large or 16 small muffin tins. In a bowl, mix together well egg, milk and oil. Set aside. On a piece of wax paper, sift together flour, baking powder, salt and 1/2 cup sugar. The banana can be mashed in a little bowl or squished by hand in a small plastic bag. Mix ingredients alternately in the first bowl, trying not to mix too much (Large holes will form when the muffin is cooked if batter is mixed too much.) Fill the greased muffin tins 3/4 full. Mix nuts, cinnamon and sugar together and sprinkle on top of each uncooked muffin. Bake 15 to 20 minutes until muffins are lightly browned and pull away from the edge of tin. Serve hot.

❖ Special note: Store in plastic wrap or freezer bags. Freeze until ready to use. Be careful when reheating in the microwave.

Coffee Break Blueberry Muffins

(Circa 1956)

1 egg
1 cup milk
1/4 cup salad oil
2 cups sifted bread flour
1/2 cup sugar
3 teaspoons baking powder
1 teaspoon salt
1/2 to 1 cup frozen or fresh blueberries
2 tablespoons sugar
1/4 teaspoon cinnamon

❖ Preheat oven to 450° F and grease 12 muffin tins. Beat the egg slightly with a fork and stir in milk and salad oil. Sift together flour, 1/2 cup sugar, baking powder and salt. Add this and blueberries to egg mixture stirring only just enough to moisten. Put in muffin tins. Mix together sugar and cinnamon, sprinkle on top of each muffin. Bake for 20 to 25 minutes. Makes about 12 muffins.

The Coffee Break

Just outside the main gate on Upper College Road—some of you might even remember—was the old Evans Market. Well, right next to it, just a hole in the wall, was one of the University's special haunts...THE COFFEE BREAK which was run by several professors' wives, who, without a doubt, were the best at what they did—Make coffee an... These blueberry muffins were the BEST...unfortunately I can not credit the cooks by name but here is the recipe which they were willing to share with me as a freshman foods major at URI. I have made them many times and shared the recipe even more...hope you enjoy.

Blueberry Cream Muffins

This is the recipe which won The Blue Ribbon at the Washington County Fair in 1992...I'm sure you'll agree that this recipe is a prize winner.

4 eggs
1 cup vegetable oil
1 teaspoon vanilla
2 cups sugar
4 cups flour
1 teaspoon salt
2 teaspoons baking powder
1 teaspoon baking soda
2 cups sour cream
2 cups fresh blueberries

❖ Preheat oven 400° F for 20 minutes. Beat together eggs, oil and vanilla. Sift together dry ingredients and add alternately with sour cream to creamed mixture. Fold in blueberries. Put in muffin tins. Bake 18 to 20 minutes.
Makes 2 dozen.

Caramel Pecan Muffins

1/3 cup brown sugar
2 tablespoons butter
1/2 cup pecans
1 cup flour
1/4 cup sugar
3 teaspoons baking powder
1/2 teaspoon salt
1/4 cup shortening
1 cup oatmeal, uncooked
1 beaten egg
1 cup milk

❖ Combine brown sugar with soft butter. Put in muffin tins and arrange pecan halves in each.

❖ In separate bowl mix flour, sugar, baking powder and salt. Cut in shortening; blend in oats; lightly stir in egg and milk.

❖ Fill muffin tins 2/3 full. Bake in a preheated 425° F oven for about 20 minutes. Remove immediately from muffin pans.
Makes 12 to 15 muffins.

Pecan Rolls

2 cups flour
2 teaspoons baking powder
1/2 teaspoon salt
1 tablespoon sugar
3 tablespoons shortening
3/4 cup milk
Margarine
Brown sugar
3/4 cup pecans, chopped

❖ Mix flour, baking powder, salt and sugar. Cut in shortening until it looks like corn meal. Add milk and mix lightly with a fork to form a soft dough. Make into a ball and pat flat on a floured surface to 1/4-inch thick rectangle. Dot with margarine and sprinkle with brown sugar and chopped nuts. Roll up like a jelly roll and cut into 3/4 to 1-inch thick slices. Place close together on a greased 9 inch pan. Bake in 400° F oven about 12 to 15 minutes.

Dora's Sour Cream Coffee Cake

3 cups flour
1/2 teaspoon salt
1 tablespoon baking powder
1 teaspoon baking soda
1/2 pound butter or margarine
1 cup sugar
3 eggs
1 teaspoon vanilla
8 ounces sour cream
1/2 cup chopped nuts
1/2 cup sugar
1 to 2 teaspoons cinnamon
3/4 cup blueberries, optional

❖ Sift together flour, salt, baking powder and baking soda. In another bowl, cream together softened butter with 1 cup sugar. Beat until fluffy. Add eggs 1 at a time to creamed mixture. Beat well, then add vanilla. Alternately mix dry ingredients with creamed mixture and sour cream. Set aside. Mix nuts, 1/2 cup sugar and cinnamon well. Grease a large 9 or 10-inch tube pan. Pour 1/2 of batter into tube pan. Add topping and blueberries, if using. Pour in remainder of batter. Decorate with whole nuts on top, if desired. Bake at 350° F for 60 minutes, not a minute longer. Cool thoroughly in pan or it will break. Cool about 2 hours.

Dough Boys

Young bride's method from my grandmother's old receipt book...1910

❖ Buy at the baker's 2 pounds bread dough, cut into pieces a little larger than an egg. Press flat between finger and thumb. Let rise a little on a floured board. Fry in deep fat or drippings until brown and, when pierced, no dough is left clinging to fork. Serve with butter and salt, as a bread.

Italian Doughboys

Oil
1 pound fresh Italian bread dough
1 cup ricotta cheese
1 cup shredded mozzarella cheese

❖ Take a piece of dough about the size of an egg. Stretch it with your fingers until it is reasonably flat and about 5 inches around. Place a teaspoon of ricotta and a teaspoon of shredded mozzarella into the center of the dough. Add a sprinkle of salt and pepper. Fold the dough over the mixture so that it encases the cheeses. Pinch the edges with a fork or your fingers so that the cheese won't leak out. Put 1 quart of oil into a saucepan and bring to bubbling. Drop the doughboys one at a time into the hot fat. When one side is golden brown, about two minutes, flip it over and let the other side brown. Remove with a slotted spoon and drain on a paper towel. Sprinkle with sugar.

❖ Note: These can be made without cheese and served with sugar, popular at all kinds of festivals.

The Jonnycake Controversy

The Great Controversy

Differing opinions on the subject of jonnycakes—their spelling and texture—cannot be lightly treated or worse, ignored. However, we must be aware that some unenlightened readers may not be aware of the controversy or even of jonnycakes. So here goes.

Jonnycakes, Johnnycakes or Journeycakes?

Flint corn and jonnycakes are a claim to fame for the state of Rhode Island and Providence plantations. They have been an important part of our state for almost 350 years When Roger Williams arrived in the area in 1636, he found the Indians growing flint corn, and it became one of the main food crops for Indians and Colonists alike.

According to one version, in the fall the Indians moved back into the foothills, among the fir trees, and built their winter wigwams and covered them with the bark of white cedar. As the Indians traveled, they made up little cornmeal cakes for lunches. These were known as *journey-cakes*. When the English began copying them, they smoothed the *word* out as "*jarney,*" and then to "*jonny*" and now they are known as the **Rhode Island jonny-cakes.**

Regarding the various spellings of "*jonny-cake*" and their origin, Miss Audrey R. Duckert, of the staff of Webster's New International Dictionary; states "There is sufficient evidence to conjecture (but not enough to prove) that both '*johnnycake*' and '*journey-cake*' are from an earlier '*jonakin,*' which first appeared in print in 1675. The first printed record we have for '*jonnycake*' is 1739; for '*journeycake,*' 1754."

Miss Duckert goes on to state that *journeycake* refers to a hard cake intended to last throughout a long trip. Or, perhaps the Shawnee Indian cake that trappers in Maryland learned to make became "**Shawneecake**" and then became known as "*jonnycake,*" As to the "*h*" in *johnnycake,*

Vermonters refer to corn bread as *johnnycake* and, since Rhode Islanders call it corn bread, there is ample reason to call the Rhode Island corn-cake "*jonnycake.*"

RI Legislature Makes Final Decision

Whatever the spelling, a true jonny-cake must be made with "whitecap flint corn. "To set the rules for this native food, the Rhode Island legislature in the 1940s decided that only those made with flint corn may be labeled "Rhode Island Jonnycakes." White flint corn can only be grown successfully in the Island area. A uniqueness of nature rules. Soil and climate conditions and original seed and propagation in this same area is important for the purity of this variety of corn. For example, those who have tried to grow flint corn in other areas of the country have been unable to have a successful 2nd or 3rd generation seed. Our ancestors, while they could not improve the corn itself, did improve upon the methods of grinding the corn, and soon windmills were erected for the sole purpose of grinding corn, most using granite stones, thus the name stone ground meal. Early documentation tells about farmers sharing these modern inventions of the grist mill which produced a quality product at The Old Mill in Nantucket, on Prudence Island, Jamestown, in South County and in Newport County. Still operating are the mills called Palmer, Gray's, Carpenter's who grow only white flint corn and the one known worldwide, Kenyon's. At the opening of Epcot (Disneyworld) in France, Kenyon's was used in the U.S. Pavilion. Many of those in the northeast tried their first johnny-cake, at Kenyon's booth in the Rhode Island Building (displays Rhode Island Products) at the Eastern State Exposition, West Springfield, Massachusetts.

Blame the "Indians"

One thing is certain, white flint corn and primitive jonnycakes were certainly

as American as apple pie and were introduced to the Pilgrims in 1620. Miles Standish discovered a cache where the Indians had stored some of their harvest of corn. This grain was unknown to them, but Squanto, a Putexet Indian who was friendly towards them, taught them how to pound the corn into a meal with a crude mortar and pestle and then how to mix it with water into a stiff dough. It was spread on a small flat surface and stood before an open fire and cooked into a sort of cake, and here we have the original jonnycake. It is clear that the original jonnycakes were thick affairs as were Phillis' cakes in "The Johnnycake Papers" by Thomas Robinson Hazard.

The Jonny-cake Papers

Phillis, after taking from the chest her modicum of meal, proceeded to boil through her finest sieve, reserving the first teacupful for the especial purpose of powdering fish before being fried. After sifting the meal she proceeded to carefully knead it in a wooden tray, having first scalded it with boiling water, and added sufficient fluid,

sometimes new mill, at other times pure water, to make it proper consistence. It was then placed on a jonny-cake board about three-quarters of an inch in thickness, and well-dressed on the surface with rich cream to keep it from blistering when placed before the fire. The cake was then placed upright on the hearth before a bright, green hardwood fire supported by a heart-shaped flat-iron. First, the flat's front smooth surface was placed immediately against the back of the jonny-cake board to hold it in a perpendicular position before the fire until the main part of the cake was sufficiently baked. Then the flat-iron was turned so as to support the board in a reclining position until the bottom and top extremities of the cake were in turn baked, and lastly the board was slewed round and rested partly against the handle of the flat-iron. When the jonny-cake was sufficiently done on the first side, a knife was passed between it and the board, and it was dexterously turned and anointed, as before, with sweet, golden-tinged cream, previous to being again placed before the fire.

Through Thick and Thin

The jonnycake controversy will probably continue on a healthy and well for many years to come. Helping perpetuate the debate are a number of breakfast festivals, individuals and companies serving up their special versions of this delicious specialty. As you can see from recipes, Island people enjoy them for breakfast, lunch and dinner, thick or thin, with or without milk, or egg etc., served with maple syrup, butter and salt, Cheddar cheese, cream dried beef, dark Karo, butter and sugar or even plain. My mother always served them with Scotch ham and a milk gravy. Served in several restaurants in the area, they remain popular, particularly at Dove Crest in West Greenwich, an authentic American Indian restaurant in "Arcadia" and Nantucket's "The Overlook" where they are shaped like whales for young eaters at breakfast time.

Boyd's Famous Thick Jonnycakes

This is another once upon a time story...I found this old recipe sheet in my grandmother's cookbook. I have been unable to find out its exact vintage but one clue is the telephone number Ports. 385-W-3 for Boyd Brothers, Portsmouth, Rhode Island.

The recipes are a little different also. Use this meal to fry fish.

1½ cups cornmeal
Egg, optional
1½ teaspoons salt

❖ Scald cornmeal with either hot milk or water. Mix smooth. Thin slightly with milk. Drop by spoonfuls on hot, lightly greased iron griddle. Fry slowly until nicely browned on both sides. Serve at once. Serves 3.

❖ Many people on Block Island use this recipe.

Brown and Hopkins Country Store

In the heart of the Chepachet Historic District, a rural western Rhode Island village, a place of real character, is home to Brown and Hopkins Country Store. It is said to be "the oldest continually running store in the United States," since 1809. It recently has changed ownership, but Claudia Amaral, proprietress, promises the store will be essentially the same as it's been in the past, with its unique mix of delicacies and antiques, its penny candy and its friendly hometown atmosphere." On the original shelves, or in the cracker barrel near the pot bellied stove, are likely to be found today many of the foods the 19th century residents of the village enjoyed, featuring real "rat cheese," homemade breads and its "light lunch menu." There's something for everyone here.

Festival Time

South County Festival

Another festival of note is held each August at the South County Museum in Narragansett at Canonchet Farm, where the controversy goes on according to Richard Donnelly of North Kingstown. Should the jonny cake be thick—South County style or thin and crisp, Newport style?

Jonnycake Storytelling Festival

Each September, this festival attracts people from all over the East. Sponsored by the South Kingstown Recreation Commission and the Rhode Island State Council for the Arts Storytelling of all types are featured—from ghost stories to workshops on storytelling. But the Sunday Morning Jonnycake Brunch O'Stories is most popular and of course jonnycakes are served. Since this is South County, expect them to be thick.

Newport-Style Thin Jonnycake

1 cup white corn meal
1/2 teaspoon salt
2 teaspoons sugar
1³/4 cup milk

❖ Put ingredients in bowl, mix thoroughly and cook on a well-greased, hot griddle, as you would griddle cakes. Add extra milk if necessary to keep mixture thin. Some prefer to omit the sugar.

❖ Note: Always keep your stone-ground products in the refrigerator or freezer.

Thin Jonnycakes

The meal is not scalded for these cakes.

1 cup corn meal
1¹/4 cups cold milk
1 teaspoon salt

❖ Mix to a smooth batter. Drop slowly by spoonfuls, onto lightly greased iron griddle. Let brown; turn and brown the other side. Serve at once.

Brown and Hopkins Thick Jonnycakes

"An olde receipt"

1 cup Rhode Island cornmeal
1/2 teaspoon salt
1 teaspoon sugar
1 tablespoon butter
1¹/2 cups boiling water
Cream or rich milk

❖ Put dry ingredients and butter in a heavy saucepan; add boiling water gradually, mixing thoroughly. Thin with cream or milk. Continue stirring while cooking over low heat for 10 to 15 minutes, until mixture looks like mashed potato. Drop by teaspoonfuls onto hot greased griddle. Cook until brown, turn and finish browning. Serve piping hot with butter. Serves 4.

The May Breakfast

I grew up with jonnycakes as a family staple. Some years ago, we wouldn't say how many...I joined the "line of jonnycake makers" at the North Scituate Baptist Church. Well, as years went on and with attrition taking its toll, I became chairman of the jonnycakes at the Annual May Breakfast. The worst thing about the job is the "heat" (It may be a "little like purgatory," but fortunately with my beliefs, this is as close as I will get to it), and the best part about this job is the greatest volunteers ever from our community. My husband Carl, who is in charge of mixing a minimum of 75 pounds of meal in only 4 hours, is ably assisted by John Gorham, and my lifesavers, Jim and Paul Winfield, Emily Barrett, Alberta Hopkins, Don Harris and so many, many others. I thank them in more ways than one.

Just Right!

To those who continue the propagation of the jonnycake controversy, the prize goes to Walt Pulaski, who brings all his friends to the Annual

May Breakfast at the North Scituate Baptist Church and then stands on "his tradition that jonnycakes must be thin." People come from far and wide for May Breakfasts that feature jonnycakes and for those not familiar with them we say, no they're not a pancake, a waffle, a fritter, an English muffin or a hush puppy. They're a jonnycake. Hope you get to try them either thick or thin. By the way, come May Breakfast time each year, says the committee: **"They're neither thick nor thin, they're just right."** Hope to see you there and we may serve 800 this year!

My Jonnycakes

1 cup white cornmeal
1/2 teaspoon salt
2 teaspoons sugar
1½ cups boiling water
Milk
Bacon fat, preferably (if not shortening)

❖ In a medium bowl, mix cornmeal, salt and sugar. Add about 1½ cups boiling water, all at once and stir constantly, until well mixed. If mixture is too thick, gradually add enough milk so that mixture can be dropped by a heaping tablespoonful on a hot greased griddle. (My grandmother always used a spider. The secret is enough fat and a very thick, heavy pan that holds even heat.) The secret in dropping the jonnycakes is "in your wrist." Cook for 5 to 6 minutes on first side and don't pat or play with them, when edges are brown turn once and let cook until lightly brown on other side. Serve immediately.

Stone Grist Mill

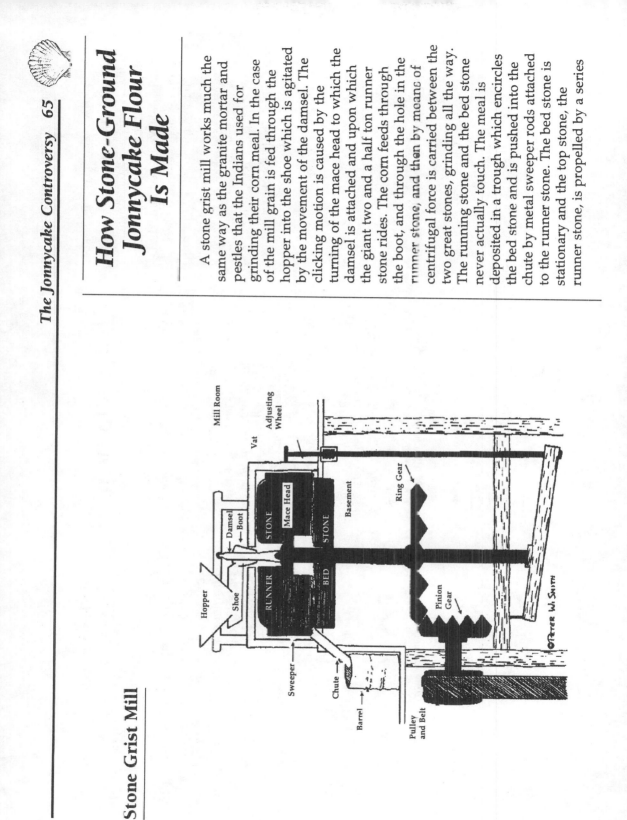

Mill Room

Vat

Adjusting Wheel

Damsel

Boot

STONE

Mace Head

STONE

Basement

Ring Gear

Hopper

Shoe

RUNNER

BED

Pinion Gear

Sweeper

Chute

Barrel

Pulley and Belt

© Peter W. Smith

How Stone-Ground Jonnycake Flour Is Made

A stone grist mill works much the same way as the granite mortar and pestles that the Indians used for grinding their corn meal. In the case of the mill grain is fed through the hopper into the shoe which is agitated by the movement of the damsel. The clicking motion is caused by the turning of the mace head to which the damsel is attached and upon which the giant two and a half ton runner stone rides. The corn feeds through the boot, and through the hole in the runner stone, and then by means of centrifugal force is carried between the two great stones, grinding all the way. The running stone and the bed stone never actually touch. The meal is deposited in a trough which encircles the bed stone and is pushed into the chute by metal sweeper rods attached to the runner stone. The bed stone is stationary and the top stone, the runner stone, is propelled by a series of belts, pulleys, and gears. To accommodate the different grain sizes, the miller is able to adjust the gap between the stones by means of a lever upon which the central shaft rests. The movement of the adjusting wheel moves the runner stone away from or closer to the bed stone. "By keeping his nose to the grindstone" the miller can detect the smell of granite which indicates that the stones are too close.

Kenyon Corn Meal

Which brings us to Usquepaugh, a South County mill village, which is now home to the Kenyon Corn Meal Company. Usquepaugh, an Indian name meaning "good whiskey" probably "good cider" was a major export with johnnycake meal in its early operation. The original grist mill operated as a woolen mill on the Queen's River in the 1840s. In 1909, Mr. Charles D. Kenyon, postmaster and owner of the village store purchased the grist mill and was soon supplying 25 and 50-pound sacks to local grocers in South County. Charles Kenyon died in 1938, and the business passed to his son, who was unable to carry on the business. Ownership has passed several times and finally in 1971, to its present-day owner, Paul E.T. Drumm, Jr. who, with the help of Charlie Walmsley who had been the miller for many years, (I first met Charlie in 1956 and got the finest tour of any business operation of my life.) continued a thriving operation. Mr. Drumm established the mill store and the gift foods business and has developed many new stone ground products. In 1974, the village under the auspices of the Kenyon Corn Meal Company, began hosting the Usquepaugh Johnny Cake Festival. The festival is now run by a committee and includes family events and a large parade.

Courtesy Kenyon Corn Meal Company, Usquepaugh, Rhode Island

Farms and Barnyards

Blanchard Farm

"Apple Country" in the western hills of Rhode Island is a farm which has been operating for 5 generations as full-time farmers. It all started in the 1860s with John Blanchard, then Charles, then Herbert, then Ben, then Herbert, Sr., then Herbert, Jr. and last but not least, Herbert the 2nd, otherwise known as "Sonny." In the early days of this farm 75 or more Holsteins could be found in residence. Besides milk, John and Charles sold wood and lumber. The first orchard, with apples, pears and quince was established about 1923; vegetables were added in the 30s and peaches in the 50s. A white peach, called "Champion," is one of the best varieties to be enjoyed from this orchard. Few farms now have customers waiting as Blanchard's does in early summer for the first picking. "Got any corn yet, Herb?"

Despite woodchucks, raccoons and other varmints, the Blanchards have survived. Sonny branched out in the late 70s with his Fruit and Deli part of the family stand and includes "corn

beef equal to none." He "corns" his own beef using his grandfather's recipe. His fruit baskets are probably the most interesting in the area featuring fruits and products from the area including honey.

Blanchard Farm
Peach or Quince Pudding

- 2 cups flour
- 2 teaspoons baking powder
- 1/2 teaspoon salt
- 1 egg, beaten
- 1 cup milk
- 2 tablespoons margarine, melted

❖ 1 cup quince or peach preserves

Sift together flour, baking powder and salt. Stir in beaten egg, milk, and margarine to form a stiff batter. Add the preserves, beat thoroughly. Turn into a well-buttered shallow baking dish or pie plate. Bake at 350° F for 25 to 30 minutes. Cut into 6 pieces and serve with sweetened whipped cream or topping.

Blanchard Farm
Baked Apple Dumplings

- 1 recipe 9-inch pie pastry
- 6 baking apples, cored, peeled
- Sugar, cinnamon and margarine

❖ Roll and cut pastry into six 5-inch squares. Place apples in center of each square. Fill apples with sugar, and a little cinnamon, and a dot of margarine. Wet edges of pastry with water and draw opposite corners together; pinch together. Place on baking sheet. Bake at 450° F for 10 minutes; reduce heat to 350° F and bake for 20 to 30 minutes or until apples are tender. Serve with Rumford Hard Sauce (see page 144). Makes 6 dumplings.

❖ Note: These recipes are adaptations of recipes from early editions of the Rumford Complete Cookbook, published by the Rumford Chemical Works, makers of baking powder and other products since 1854. Not only did Rumford give the country its first baking powder, it was one of the first companies to issue booklets and folders on cooking. It now distributes from Terre Haute, Indiana.

Morning Glory Farm

All produce is grown on their 55 plus acres in Edgartown, Martha's Vineyard, according to Jim and Debbie Athearn. Morning Glory Farm operates from April to Thanksgiving, employing 30 to 35 people. Their retail outlet is a roadside stand familiar to all in the area. Featured are strawberries, blueberries, peas, beans, potatoes, squash, peppers, Island lettuce, herbs, corn and fresh and dried flowers.

Morning Glory Farm
Dilly Beans

4 pounds green beans

Brine:

3 cups white vinegar
4 tablespoons salt
3 cups water

❖ Wash and trim beans to fit standing up in pint canning jars, about 3/4 inch below lid. To make brine, bring vinegar, salt and water to a good boil. Sterilize jars and add the following to each one:

2 teaspoons dill seed
1 dill head (for color)
1/2 teaspoon mustard seed
1/4 teaspoon crushed red hot pepper or 3 whole black peppercorns
2 cloves garlic, peeled

❖ Pack jars tightly with beans. Pour hot brine over beans to cover. Leave 1/2 inch headspace. Clean jar lip and edge. Seal with lids. Process for 7 minutes in boiling water bath.

Morning Glory Farm
Zucchini Bread

1 cup zucchini purée
1/2 cup canola oil
1 1/2 teaspoons vanilla
2 eggs
3/4 cup unbleached white flour
3/4 cup whole wheat flour
1 cup sugar
1/8 teaspoon salt
1/2 teaspoon baking soda
1/4 teaspoon baking powder
1/2 teaspoon cinnamon

❖ Blend together zucchini, oil, vanilla and eggs. In a separate bowl, sift together remaining ingredients. Combine the 2 mixtures thoroughly. Fill 1 ungreased 5x9-inch bread pan. Bake at 350° F for about 1 hour.

Morning Glory Farm
Gazpacho

3 green peppers, seeded and quartered
2 medium onions, quartered
10 cloves garlic
1/2 cup each fresh parsley and cilantro
1 lemon, juice only
2 limes, juice only
1/4 cup (or more) fresh basil
1 teaspoon cumin
2 tablespoons Tabasco sauce
1/4 cup olive oil
1/2 teaspoon pepper
1 teaspoon salt
1/4 cup wine vinegar
4 medium cucumbers, peeled, seeded
1 tablespoon honey
6 cups (or more) seeded tomatoes
1 or 2 cups tomato juice

❖ Pulse first 16 ingredients in food processor. Add tomatoes and pulse. Stir in tomato juice and chill.

Salisbury Farm

Established by Squire Williams Salisbury in the mid 1800s, the Salisbury Farm lies in the tranquil hills of western Johnston. Originally the farm supplied dairy and forage products to area residents and the Providence to Plainfield stage coach line. Although still providing quality forage products, the farm operated today by Wayne and Lois Salisbury now emphasizes pick-your-own strawberries, sweet corn and pumpkins.

Catering to both individuals and groups, a visit to the farm in June will be both interesting, and educational and, for some, extremely nostalgic.

Salisbury Farm
Frozen Strawberry Daiquiris

1 6-ounce can frozen limeade
    concentrate
1½ to 2 cups frozen strawberries
6 ounces light rum
8 to 10 ice cubes
1 teaspoon confectioners' sugar

❖ Put all ingredients, except ice in blender. Blend well and add ice cubes, 2 or 3 at a time until all cubes are used and mixture is frozen to a mush. Pour into frosted glasses and garnish with a sprig of mint and a fresh strawberry, if available.

Seldom Seen Farm

Seldom Seen Farm is an 160-acre farm located in Harmony, Rhode Island. The house is an Evans Farm House, circa 1790. Winifred Thompson and Marcus Thompson, Sr. purchased this house, barn and farm land from the heirs of Myltilla Steere. Presently, the family raise Hampshire, Southdown, Dorset and Cheviot sheep for show, wool and meat.

Seldom Seen is certainly in the woods as they would say in Rhode Island. Off the beaten track, they are famous for their "show animals" which can be seen at shows throughout the northeast and particularly at the "Big E" in Springfield, Massachusetts, at the end of September each year. Not only do they participate as exhibitor's but run the "whole show" in the Wool Barn, where you see sheep from fur to finish. A little story aside, my hubby lost his favorite friend one fall, and I decided to get a new one. Seldom Seen came to the rescue. I had my chance to choose anyone I wanted at the barn—a sheep you thought! Well, needless to say, I fell in love with a chubby two month old kitten with eyes as big as saucers, long whiskers and a little black body with white tummy and boots. Well, this was Chrissy, who was Seldom Seen's Christmas present to us.

Believe it or not, I didn't like lamb until I had Seldom Seen lamb and used some of their recipes—hope you enjoy them as much as we have.

Seldom Seen Farm
Fresh Mint Sauce for Lamb

2 cups minced fresh mint
3 tablespoons boiling water
2 tablespoons sugar
3 tablespoons dry white wine or
  white wine vinegar

❖ Put minced mint in a small bowl
and pour boiling water over mint.
Let stand for 20 minutes. Mix
together sugar and wine until dissolved and add to mint. Stir well
and serve with lamb or any meat
dish. Makes 3/4 cup.

❖ Note: Store in sterilized jars if
making more than one batch. Cover
with a thin layer of paraffin.

Seldom Seen Farm
Coffee-Sauced Roast Lamb

1 leg of lamb
Salt and pepper
Dry mustard
1 cup strong black coffee
2 tablespoons cream
2 tablespoons sugar
3 tablespoons brandy

❖ Salt and pepper leg of lamb and
dust all over with dry mustard.
Roast at 300° F for 18 minutes per
pound. When cooked internal
temperature should be 140° using
meat thermometer. Combine black
coffee, cream, sugar and brandy
and baste lamb frequently.

Seldom Seen Farm
Lamb Chops in Foil

*So easy, any one will become the
"Chief of the Day."*

❖ For each serving allow:

2 lamb chops
1 sliced zucchini, unpeeled
1 small tomato, quartered
1 small onion, sliced
Small green pepper, cored and sliced
Dash of basil
Salt and pepper
Garlic powder

❖ Make a packet with the above in
each, wrapped tightly. Grill on low
about 25 to 30 minutes. Be sure to
turn several times. Another great
way to use this recipe is to bake at
350° F for 1 1/4 to 1 1/2 hours.

Seldom Seen Farm
Lamb Porcupines

1 1/2 pounds ground lamb
1 cup uncooked rice
1 egg
3 tablespoons parsley
1 teaspoon dill weed
1 teaspoon garlic salt
1/4 teaspoon pepper
2 cups tomato juice
3 cups water

❖ Mix together first 7 ingredients and
form into balls. Place in a large
saucepan and cover with tomato
juice and water.

❖ Simmer, covered, for 45 to 50
minutes. Add additional water
if necessary.

❖ Note: For a full dinner you may put
sliced onions, peppers and carrots
in bottom of pan. Put balls on top of
vegetables, then add liquid.

Thimble Farm

Thimble Farm was founded in 1982 by a couple who wanted to change their vocation as well as their way of life, and get away from it all—a 50-acre farm in the Vineyard with "pick your own" raspberries and strawberries. In a few years, currants, blueberries and huckleberries will complete this fine line of small fruits. Bud says, "We have the best honeydew melons anywhere." A 12-month operation, Thimble Farm supplies the island with tomatoes from its computerized Dutch-style greenhouses year round. Flowers and other produce are sold wholesale and retail. Bud and Patricia Moskow certainly seem happy. Now that they have gotten away from it all—to quote Pat, "we have never been so busy!"

Thimble Farm
Raspberry Vinegar

3 quarts raspberries
1 quart white wine vinegar
1 tablespoon (or to taste) sugar

❖ In stainless steel bowl, add enough sugar to vinegar to remove some of the bite. Add 1 quart raspberries and let sit for 24 hours. Strain berries, reserving vinegar. Add another quart of berries and let stand another 24 hours. Strain again, add third quart of berries and store in tightly sealed bottles. Use in vinaigrettes. It goes particularly well with fruit salads. An interesting Christmas gift.

Mary's Thimble Farm
Strawberry Bread

3 cups flour
1/2 teaspoon salt
1 teaspoon baking soda
2 cups sugar
1 tablespoon cinnamon
3 eggs, beaten
1 cup oil
2 to 2 1/2 cups sliced (fresh or frozen) strawberries

❖ In a mixing bowl, combine first 5 ingredients. Mix well. Combine eggs, oil and strawberries in a separate bowl. Add to dry ingredients and mix well. Pour into greased and floured 9x5-inch loaf pan. Bake at 350° F for 1 hour or until loaf tests done. Freezes well.

Future Farmers
of America

Well, since you've heard about 4-H throughout this book, now we'll let you in on the other half of the coin which I feel helps to make some of the best young men and women in the Islands. I've competed against, judged, harassed, taught and finally became one of them at Scituate Junior/Senior High School. In 1972, I became an Honorary member of the Scituate Chapter of FFA and in 1988, was named to their Hall of Fame. Chapter Advisor, David Lewis, in our interview says that "without a doubt the Annual FFA Parent and Member Banquet is the highlight of the year for members past and present." One of the keys to success is Planning. The members prepare and serve the entire meal to 150 plus guests with the help of advisors and alumni, who come back every year to assist with the

A Farmer's Best Friend—

...that is what Dr. John Beck, veterinarian, was for almost 40 years in Rhode Island and Connecticut. He was well known for his farm visits, especially at breakfast time.

Beck's Best Breakfast

7 slices firm bread, lightly buttered
1 cup grated sharp Cheddar cheese
1/2 pound mushrooms, sautéed in butter
1 pound pork sausage, cooked, drained
2 cups milk
1 teaspoon salt
1/2 teaspoon paprika
1/2 teaspoon dry mustard
7 eggs

❖ Line bottom of 9x13-inch baking dish with bread. Sprinkle with cheese, mushrooms and cooked sausage. Beat milk, salt, paprika, dry mustard and eggs together.

recipe continued on page 74

FFA Shopping List for Chicken Barbecue for 150

3 boxes whole chicken (70 pounds each) must be cut up!
6 gallons barbecue sauce
20 pounds shell macaroni
5 gallons tomato sauce
Parmesan cheese
100 count potatoes
3 number 10 cans peas
3 number 10 cans carrots or corn
5 cases lettuce
Celery sticks 3   5 # packages
Carrot sticks 3   5 # packages
10 pounds tomatoes
2 gallons Italian salad dressing
30 dozen rolls
2 # 10 cans cranberry sauce
3 commercial size sheet cakes
1 pound coffee
4 gallons milk
18 gallons punch
25 bags charcoal, Charcoal lighter
500 paper platters

preparations. Two of these dedicated persons are Wayne Salisbury and Bob Cuniff. Not only is the food great, but Proficiency Awards are presented to students in Vocational Agriculture, grades 9 to 12 for outstanding work in agriculture and related areas, which include public speaking. Well, we haven't got a recipe for the Chicken Barbecue, but they provided us with a shopping list, which for 150 persons will probably be of more help than a recipe...The entire membership gets ready the week before...building the barbecue pit outside the school cafeteria, shopping, preparing and last minute details and of course nerves...and you think all teenagers want to eat is pizza! P.S. Mary thanks and a hurrah to an unsung volunteer of the school, Mary Babliowiecz, manager school lunch, who never says no to the student body.

The Scituate Art Festival brings literally thousands to town on Columbus Day week who must also be fed. Local organizations pitch in to help the festival and for their local fund raising. The FFA have an Apple Shed where they sell fresh apples, hot and cold cider...For each gallon of cider, add 1 apple that has been pierced with 3 cinnamon sticks, 1 tablespoon of ground cinnamon and some nutmeg. Dave says, "It tastes better the longer it cooks."

Pour over top of sausage, cover and refrigerate overnight. Bake, un-covered, at 350° F for 25 minutes or until set. Cut into slices or squares and serve with a wedge of melon or other fruit.

❖ Note: May substitute ½ cup skim mozzarella for Cheddar cheese; margarine for butter; turkey sausage for pork sausage; skim milk for whole milk; ¼ cup egg substitute for each egg in recipe. Cooking time is about the same as for regular recipe.

S & S Farms

When is a farm not a farm? When it's a pseudonym! My father always considered himself a small farmer. We had a roadside stand where we sold vegetables and flowers retail, as well as potatoes and corn to the wholesale market. We had only a few pigs for our family use and, on the average, 500 to 1,000 broilers and laying hens. Not a large operation at all, even for Rhode Island. My mother and I sold chickens to the Providence marketplace during the Second World War and for about 10 years afterwards. Needless to say, I had a poultry project in 4-H, both production and as a foods project, as well as being named a National Junior Vegetable Grower.

As we got older, our farming projects decreased to just vegetables for our own use. My father, was innovative, decided to fund his garden after he retired. He called himself "Farmer Sherman" and charged customers $25 to $35 a year for summer vegetables. Each week, he would take the "pick of the crop" in season and fill a half bushel basket to deliver to his customers. All remarked "what a buy!" At the same time, my husband and I had a substantial garden which also included raspberries, strawberries and some vegetables that my father's didn't.

A number of years ago, we wanted to once again go into competition. Well, there were no categories other than 4-H and commercial farmers available. Therefore, I made up the name S & S Farms, (Stetson and Sherman), a pseudonym. We entered in the commercial farmers division at the state and county fairs and that year we received the top prize for our entry. Oh, how the fair buzzed trying to find out "who this S & S Farms was" to no avail. We never did enter competition again, but have through the years donated our produce and farm products to local charitable events and all of our jams, jellies and other specialties for gift giving have a special label which says, Specialty of S & S Farms.

S & S Farms Country Christmas Dinner

For many years my family had a roast loin of pork for Christmas dinner—not only was it tradition, but of pure Yankee frugality. We raised our own pigs, so we always had a full loin saved for Christmas from the October slaughter. Remember in days gone by slaughtering was not done until the first frost. Thank goodness times have changed in this respect, but for some reason pork doesn't taste the same as it did, although it is better for you. Now known as the other white meat, it has approximately the same calories and amount of fat as the same size serving of white meat poultry—prepared by the same method.

Menu

Crown Roast of Pork with
Sausage Stuffing
Applesauce — Gravy
Roasted Potatoes
Boiled Onions
Butternut Squash
Turnips — Green Peas
Rolls — Pumpkin Pie
Coffee

❖ For a simple meal—canned whole white potatoes can be successfully substituted for roasted potatoes. Boiled onions are available frozen, jarred or canned. You can purchase applesauce already made and heat, add a little cinnamon and serve as an accompaniment. Heaven forbid if you ever tried to serve a pork dish at our house without applesauce,

❖ For a garnish use special cinnamon crab apples around the roast or on every loin bone and add fresh parsley.

❖ Don't forget the gravy—if your family and guests don't really want it—you need it for leftovers later on.

S & S Farms
Green Tomato Mincemeat

6 cups apples
6 cups green tomatoes, chopped
4 cups brown sugar
1¹/₃ cups cider vinegar
3 cups raisins
1 tablespoon cinnamon
1 teaspoon cloves
³/₄ teaspoon allspice
³/₄ cup margarine

❖ Put all ingredients, except margarine, in a very heavy pan. Simmer for 3 hours. Add margarine; allow to melt. Pour into canning jars. Seal and process or cool and freeze. Makes 6 pints.

❖ Note: Use 2 pints per pie.

S & S Farms
Scalloped Cheese and Eggs

1¹/₂ tablespoons butter
1¹/₂ tablespoons flour
¹/₄ teaspoon salt
¹/₈ teaspoon pepper
1 cup milk
1 teaspoon Worcestershire sauce

❖ Melt butter in a saucepan and blend in flour, salt and pepper until smooth. Cook for about 3 to 5 minutes. Add milk and Worcestershire sauce, stirring constantly, until the mixture bubbles and thickens

❖ Note: May substitute ¹/₂ cup evaporated milk plus ¹/₂ cup water for milk.

1 cup soft bread crumbs
4 hard-cooked eggs, sliced
1 cup (¹/₄ pound) grated sharp Cheddar cheese

❖ Butter a shallow 1-quart baking dish. Place half bread crumbs in bottom of baking dish. Make a layer of the sliced eggs and grated cheese. Pour sauce over casserole ingredients. Top with remaining bread crumbs. Bake at 400° F for 25 to 30 minutes until the top is brown and sauce is bubbly.

S & S Farms
Chicken Chili con Carne

This recipe is not a chili recipe at all. The Lord knows where my grandmother ever came up with the recipe but its great for more reasons than one. I can remember if at a mealtime unexpected guests showed up, she'd just add another can of peas and make more mashed potatoes. If she didn't have enough of one ingredient, she'd add more of another. Great served as a leftover on toast for a lunch or supper. Always served with cranberries of some form.

1 fowl or chicken, cut into pieces
Water to cover chicken
2 chicken bouillon cubes
1/2 cup flour or 4 tablespoons cornstarch
3 large onions
3 green or red peppers
5 large carrots or 1 16-ounce can
1 16-ounce can peas or
1 10½-ounce package frozen peas

❖ Cover chicken with water, add bouillon cubes, bring to a boil and then simmer until chicken is tender. Let cool and the next day skim

chicken fat (save to use for making gravy or may be warmed in oven or put under broiler just before serving. If you have a large group to feed, chicken will be easier to serve and will go further, if you add to gravy.

❖ Chop onion and pepper into bite-sized pieces and sauté in reserved chicken fat in large skillet until onion is transparent. Do not brown onions. Stir in flour and mix well, add chicken stock, stirring constantly until thickened and smooth. Cook carrots until slightly tender; drain. Add to chicken mixture with drained peas.

❖ Note: Gram drained the vegetables—but I cook frozen peas and fresh carrots and microwave with very little water and use the water in the gravy to save more nutrients. Serve over lots of mashed potatoes... Freezes well. Number of servings—you guess how many—depends how hungry the crowd is (at least 6).

Corn Oysters

From my research in the archives of the Nantucket Historical Society came this 1856 recipe, which believe it or not, did not have the ingredients adjusted...a real surprise, particularly because of the type of recipe which it is; as well as, the vintage. I tested it on the publisher's rep who visited one summer and much to my pleasure he had never had any version of corn oysters, corn fritters or corn cakes from New England. I won't tell you how many he ate...but it is now listed as a "a publisher's favorite." By the way, I didn't give him the recipe. I told him he'd have to buy the book, of course...

This recipe is generally made from leftover corn, although in olden times corn cut off the cob before cooking was referred to as "green corn." Serve as a bread or vegetable. Best with any kind of pork dish. I served it last with American pork sausages and apple rings accompanied by "real" maple syrup.

S & S Farms Corn Oysters

2 cups cut corn (about 6 ears) or
  1 16-ounce can whole corn
1 cup flour
4 tablespoons margarine, melted
2 eggs, beaten
3 tablespoons milk
Oil

❖ In a large bowl, lightly mix corn and flour. Stir in margarine, eggs and as much milk as needed to moisten. Do not beat.

❖ Drop by tablespoonfuls into a frying pan with about 2 to 3 tablespoons hot oil.

❖ Fry several minutes on one side and turn when brown. Do not pat. Drain on a paper towel.

❖ Makes about 12 to 14 oysters.

S & S Farms Fresh Tomato Pizza

A pizza for summer—since that's when tomatoes are best

1 pound fresh or frozen dough
1/4 cup grated Romano and Parmesan cheese
1/2 cup thinly sliced green pepper
1/2 cup thinly sliced red onion
1/4 cup chopped fresh basil or
  3 teaspoons dried
2 cups (about) thinly sliced, tomatoes, plum preferred
2 cloves garlic, minced
1 cup sliced mushrooms, optional
1 1/2 cups shredded part-skim mozzarella cheese

❖ 4 individual pizzas may be made by dividing dough into 4 equal portions. I like to use a cookie sheet. Spray lightly with cooking spray. On floured surface, pat dough into 6 to 8-inch circles or for large pizza into a rectangle to fit cookie sheet. Try not to stretch the dough, for it will shrink. If you have trouble with the dough, let it rest for several minutes. Sprinkle with Romano and Parmesan cheeses, green pepper, onion, basil, tomatoes, garlic and mushrooms. Bake in preheated 425° F oven for 25 minutes or until crust is golden brown. Sprinkle immediately with remaining mozzarella cheese. Bake just until cheese melts. Serve, it's delicious. For variety, you may want to use zucchini or broccoli which has been very lightly sautéed.

S & S Farms Snowball Dessert Buffet

A "Snowball Dessert Buffet" for winter or Christmas, with several toppings available, sugar cookies and a hot coffee, make this a do-ahead way to entertain with less stress...and your guests think it's extra special.

❖ Take an ice cream scoop and make balls with favorite flavors of slightly softened ice cream or frozen yogurt and roll them in shredded coconut and or finely chopped nuts. Put them on a metal baking pan and freeze. When frozen, store in tightly sealed plastic freezer bags and voila you're ready for a special dessert for unexpected guests or for a large party.

S & S Farms
Pumpkin Rum Bread Pudding

6½ cups dry bread crumbs from firm bread

¾ cup chopped walnuts

3 eggs, slightly beaten

1 14-ounce can condensed milk

¾ cup cooked pumpkin

1 cup cooked pumpkin

2 teaspoons cinnamon

1 teaspoon nutmeg

½ teaspoon ginger

2 cups milk

¼ cup rum or 2 teaspoons rum flavoring in ¼ cup water

¼ cup margarine, melted

2 teaspoons vanilla

Whipped cream or topping, if desired

❖ Combine bread and nuts in bottom of a buttered 12x7x2-inch baking dish. Stir together eggs, condensed milk, pumpkin, sugar and spices. Gradually stir in milk; add rum, margarine and vanilla. Pour over bread layer. Place dish in a 13x9x2-inch baking pan and fill with hot water. Bake at 350° for 1 hour or until firm. Serve warm with whipped cream. Serves 10.

S & S Farms Fresh
Strawberry Sauce

1 pint fresh strawberries

¼ cup framboise

1 cup seedless black raspberry jam

❖ Combine all ingredients in a blender or food processor and mix well. Serve with ice cream or angel food cake, chilled or at room temperature. Makes about 3 cups.

S & S Farms
Raspberry Sauce

1 cup red currant jelly or apple jelly

¼ cup rum, optional

2 cups whole raspberries or 2-ounce package frozen raspberries

❖ Heat jelly in a saucepan over very low heat. Remove from heat and stir in rum. Add raspberries and mix very gently, being careful not to crush them. Makes about 3 cups.

S & S Farms
Spiced Blueberries

1 cup apple jelly or mint jelly

1 pint blueberries or 2 cups frozen berries

¼ teaspoon ground cinnamon

¼ teaspoon ground nutmeg

¼ teaspoon lemon juice

❖ Heat jelly in a saucepan over low heat. When jelly is melted remove from heat and stir in remainder of ingredients. Makes 3 cups sauce.

Blueberries Romanoff

Simple, simple and simply delecious!

Fresh blueberries

Heavy cream, whipped or whipped topping

Nutmeg

❖ Part of the secret is to serve this dessert in a beautiful piece of glassware...example a stem wine glass or even a brandy snifter...light and refreshing and oh so easy!!!

The Whale at the Gordon Folger, Nantucket

Herbs! Herbes! or Hurbes...No Culinary Herbs...

I was introduced to a pinch of this and a pinch of that when I first watched my mother and grandmother make soup on our wood kitchen stove. A stockpot they now call it! Their collection of herbs was a combination of purchases and trade-offs with friends of a slip of this or that.

Basic herbs that you can grow on your window sill, in a pot or a plot include parsley, dill, mint, sage, chives, thyme, sweet basil, summer savory, marjoram, tarragon and oregano to mention only a few of the most popular. If you do not have a hankering for gardening or a "green thumb," most supermarkets now carry fresh herbs. If not, you can substitute dry herbs in most cases. They can be purchased at your hardware store,

plant store and seed dealer. Try some and have some fun and new flavors. Hint for those not used to cooking with herbs—use only half what the recipe calls for the first time you make the recipe. Sometimes you need to develop your palate for these new flavors.

Use herbs as an ingredient or as a garnish. Presentation (how your food looks) is great enhanced by your garnish, whether it be parsley, fruit, vegetable or relish.

Freezing your herbs: Be sure to harvest (pick) your herbs before they flower... Pick early in the day. Remove stems and any foreign matter in your selection. Dry with paper towel if needed. Put in small freezer bags and be sure to date and label. Use as fresh herbs in your recipes. Good for 6 months.

How to dry herbs in the microwave: Spread 1/2 cup fresh herbs between paper towels. Microwave on High for 2 minutes or until herbs are dried.

How to substitute fresh and dried herbs in a recipe: When herbs are dried, their flavor becomes concentrated. Therefore, 1 teaspoon of dried herbs is equivalent to 2 to 3 teaspoons of fresh herbs, depending on kind.

Tarragon Coleslaw

Something different which I had first served as an appetizer at a local steak house

1/2 head green cabbage, shredded (4 to 6 cups)
1/2 cup corn oil
1/2 cup Tarragon Vinegar (see page 80)
Garlic powder
Celery salt
Cayenne red pepper
1 teaspoon sugar

❖ Clean and shred 1/2 medium heat of cabbage with knife, grater or food processor and put in a large bowl. Sprinkle with oil and Tarragon Vinegar. Sprinkle lightly with garlic powder celery salt and red pepper. Toss thoroughly using a large spoon and fork. Taste to see if cabbage mixture is well blended at this point. Add sugar if needed. You may need more or less than 1 teaspoon depending on the flavor of cabbage. Set aside for 1/2 hour before serving. Toss again just before serving. This slaw is just as tasty the next day, even though the cabbage is not as crisp.

Tarragon Vinegar

❖ So easy! In pint jar, place one whole clove peeled garlic, and 1 spray tarragon. Cover with white vinegar. Label. Let stand at least 2 weeks before using. Trick: When vinegar bottle is empty and you don't have any fresh tarragon available, just fill again with vinegar and in another two weeks you're ready to use vinegar again. Great choice for many salads and in pork and chicken dishes, but be sure and try Tarragon Cole Slaw for a change from the mayonnaise type slaw.

Dill Butter for Fish or Meat

❖ Broil fish or meat as desired. Make an herb butter by mixing chopped fresh dill leaves with softened butter, lemon juice and a little salt. Mix well. Spread this herb butter over hot fish or meat just before serving. Makes a bland meal seem like a gourmet's delight. Try other herbs and see what your favorites are, individually or in combination with each other. Good herb combinations include basil and chives, tarragon

and chives, basil and marjoram (oregano)), parsley, chervil and chives to mention only a few interesting choices.

❖ Any of these freeze well and may be used throughout the winter as an addition to noodles, boiled or steamed vegetables in addition to above uses.

Fresh Herb Bouquets

Al Griffiths, horticulturist and Violet Higbee, nutritionist for the Extension Service of the University of Rhode Island, developed the following recipes for using herbs.

❖ Tie together 3 or more sprigs of fresh herbs with white thread or butcher's string. Place in stockpot, stew or soup the last hour of cooking. Remove herbs before serving.

Dried Herb Bags

❖ Cut cheese cloth, which can be purchased in a fabric or hardware store, into 2-inch squares. Place a .

mixture of 1 teaspoon each of parsley leaves, thyme, marjoram, 2 teaspoons celery leaves, 1/4 teaspoon sage and bay leaves on each square. Tie tightly with string. Use as you would the fresh herb bouquets.

Kitchen Potpourri

1/2 cup broken dried orange peel
1/2 cup broken dried lemon peel
1/2 cup broken dried grapefruit peel
1/2 cup dried bay leaves
1/2 cup broken cinnamon sticks
1/2 cup whole cloves
1/2 cup whole allspice
1/2 cup dried mint leaves

❖ Be sure all ingredients are well dried. Mix well and store in a tightly covered container for at least 2 weeks, shaking or mixing well each day. It should be ready after that. Put in your favorite dish and "sweet scents for you." If it is used for gift giving, seal in ziplock bags or small tightly covered jars and label. Watch at flea markets or the 5 & 10 for a small container that's just right for your potpourri gift giving.

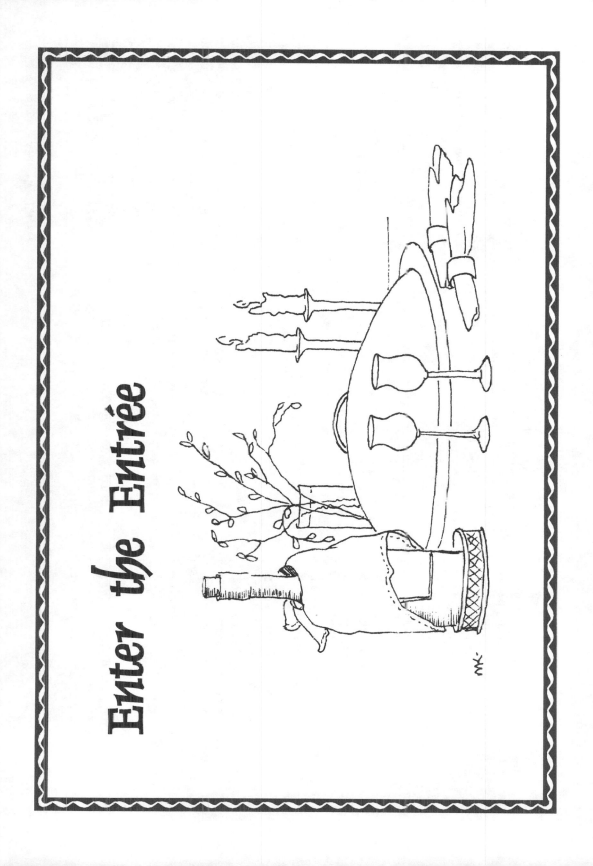

Enter the Entrée

Baked Beans

Remember baked beans have always been popular on Saturday night served with a variety of things...of course hot dogs, sometimes a small steak, hamburger fried with onions and, last but not least, codfish cakes. It also makes for a great Sunday morning breakfast or a Bean Sandwich. If you haven't tried it on toast, you're missing something. For condiments, don't forget pepper relish or piccalili, catsup or maybe mustard.

Carl's Baked Beans

This recipe is Carl's basic recipe for a pound of his famous Baked Beans, whether he uses California Pea Beans, Red Kidney or his favorite Yellow Eyes. Make your choice and follow the recipe more or less... When I do this recipe I generally bake 6 to 8 pounds of beans which saves energy in more ways than one...oven on only once, and Barbara only has to make beans every so often....Great put in the freezer and then reheated in oven or microwave on any Saturday night. Oh, I almost forgot... serve with brown bread with raisins, coleslaw or green salad and apple pie if you're lucky.

1 pound dried beans, (pea, kidney or yellow eye)
1 small onion, peeled
1 teaspoon dry mustard
1/4 teaspoon black pepper
1/2 teaspoon salt
2 shakes catsup
3/4 cup sugar
1/4 cup sugar
1/4 pound smoked bacon or salt pork

❖ Important: The night before serving you must put the beans in a large pot and cover with water. The next morning drain off the liquid and pick out any stones or foreign matter. Cover with clean water and parboil about 20 minutes on simmer until the skins start to shrivel... Drain and put in bean pot or heavy baking dish about 3 quarts.

❖ Put all ingredients in pot and then cover with hot water. Place in a 325° F oven and cook for 6 to 8 hours, checking about every 2 hours to see if you need to add more water. Do not let it get dry or the top of your beans will burn...Taste after 3 or 4 hours to see if they need more sugar, salt or syrup.

Wayne's Favorite Cowboy Beans

This is not a traditional island recipe, but one that was brought to this area by a chap "who married a native." He insists this is the best ever served with sourdough bread.

2 pounds pinto beans
2 pounds ham hocks or 1 pound lean salt pork
2 onions, chopped
4 tablespoons sugar
1/4 cup chopped chilies (canned)
1   12-ounce can tomato paste

❖ Wash beans and soak overnight. Drain, place in a large saucepan. Cover with water and parboil for 20 to 30 minutes. Drain. Add remaining ingredients and cover again with water. Put in a 350° F oven for 6 hours or more. Sample beans while cooking. Salt to taste and add water as needed.

Creamed Chipped Beef

I recently received a note from a young man who had just returned from 4-H Club National Congress in Chicago remarking that he had Creamed Chipped Beef for one of his meals. His mother said that she had it too, years before at Club Congress. Many of you who are over a certain age and were in the military have a pet name for this dish. Well, many of you I decided have never had this dish served properly, so here's the old Yankee recipe from the Islands.

One of those dishes that was inexpensive to make, served a multitude, ingredients were on hand, quick and easy...and it still is.

4 tablespoons margarine
4 tablespoons flour
1 6-ounce jar or package dried beef
2 cups milk
1/8 teaspoon salt

❖ Place fat in a saucepan or in top of double boiler. If cooked directly over flame, care must be taken not to scorch. Melt fat. Remove from heat blending in flour until smooth. Add cold milk gradually, stirring

constantly to remove all lumps. Put back on heat continuing to stir until mixture thickens and does not taste starchy. Add salt and dried beef which has been torn into pieces. Heat thoroughly in sauce and serve over johnnycakes, on toast or over mashed potatoes.

❖ Note: May substitute a can of tuna, shrimp, crab or salmon and add 1 cup cooked peas for chipped beef.

Lite Lasagna

1 to 1 1/2 pounds ground turkey
1/4 pound ground beef, optional
1 large onion, chopped
3 cloves garlic, minced
1 16-ounce can tomatoes
2 8-ounce cans tomato sauce
1 1/2 teaspoons dried basil
3/4 teaspoon dried oregano
1 egg or 1/4 cup egg substitute
2 cups low-fat cottage cheese
8 ounces low-fat Mozzarella cheese shredded
1/2 cup Parmesan cheese, divided
1 tablespoon dried parsley
1/2 tablespoon pepper
8 ounces lasagna noodles, cooked

❖ Preheat oven to 375° F. Cook turkey and ground beef with onion and garlic in skillet until brown. Drain off fat. Stir in the next 4 ingredients. Cover and let simmer for 20 to 30 minutes, stirring often.

❖ Meanwhile, beat egg and combine it with cottage cheese, Mozzarella cheese, 1/4 cup of the Parmesan cheese, parsley and pepper.

❖ In the bottom of a 9x13x2-inch baking dish, spread 1/3 of the meat sauce. Rinse noodles with hot water and layer half of them over meat sauce. Spread half of cottage cheese mixture over pasta. Repeat layers, ending with the remaining meat sauce. Sprinkle with remaining Parmesan cheese on top.

❖ Note: May be refrigerated at this point until ready to use.

❖ Bake for 35 to 45 minutes until heated through and hot and bubbly. Cover for the first half hour.

Lillian's Chili con Carne

2 ribs celery, diced
1 large onion, diced
1 small clove garlic
1 pound ground beef
1 16-ounce can tomatoes
2 cups cooked kidney beans
Salt and pepper to taste
Chili powder

❖ Fry celery, onion, garlic and ground beef until brown. Season with salt and pepper. Add can of stewed tomatoes and beans. Simmer, uncovered, for 1 hour. Add chili powder to taste. Serve Tabasco sauce on the side.

Meat-Za Pie

1 pound lean ground beef
1/2 teaspoon salt
1/4 cup dry bread crumbs
1/4 cup milk
1/2 cup tomato paste
1/2 teaspoon Italian seasoning
1/2 cup shredded sharp cheddar cheese
2 tablespoons grated Parmesan cheese

❖ Set aside 1/2 can of soup. Mix remainder of soup, ground beef, onion, egg, bread crumbs, salt and pepper together. Put this mixture in

❖ Place beef, salt, and bread crumbs in a 9-inch pan. Add milk and mixture evenly over the bottom of the pan, raising a rim about a half inch high around the side of pan. Spread tomato paste lightly over the meat mixture. Sprinkle with Italian seasoning, then with shredded cheese and grated Parmesan cheese. Bake at 400° F about 20 minutes or until cheese is melted and beef cooked. Cut in wedges and serve.

Meat and Potato Pie

1 10½-ounce can cream of mushroom soup, divided in half
1 pound ground beef
1/2 cup finely chopped onion
1 egg
1/2 cup bread crumbs
1/4 teaspoon salt
1/4 teaspoon pepper
2 cups mashed potato
1/4 cup shredded cheese

9-inch deep pie plate and bake at 350° F for 25 minutes. Then add mashed potato and shredded cheese. Top with other half of mushroom soup. Bake for another 10 to 15 minutes.

Mock Pizza

This was a very popular school lunch selection back in the 70s until packaged pizza was the new in-thing.

❖ Take 1/2 cup of favorite meatball recipe and spread on a slice of bread. Top with a little tomato paste, Italian seasoning and cheese. Bake at 400° F until meat is cooked.

Porcupine Balls

Very popular in the 40s as a great dish to stretch any budget. In the 90s it makes beef a good choice even for those on special diets because of the rice.

1 pound ground beef
1 teaspoon salt
1/4 teaspoon black pepper
1/2 cup minced onion
2/3 cup uncooked rice
2 tablespoons oil
2 1/2 cups tomato juice

❖ In a large bowl, mix beef, salt, pepper, onion and rice. Form into balls about the size of a lemon.

❖ Heat oil in large skillet, brown porcupine balls for about 15 minutes, turning occasionally to brown on all sides.

❖ Add tomato juice to skillet, cover. Cook over low heat for 45 minutes. Serves 4.

Bavarian Chops

Great with buttered noodles and green beans

2 tablespoons flour
4 boneless pork loin chops 3/4 inch thick
1 teaspoon margarine
1/2 cup chopped green onions
2 cloves garlic, minced
8 ounces mushrooms, sliced
1/2 teaspoon thyme, optional
1 8-ounce can beer, at room temperature
Salt and pepper
Minced fresh parsley, optional

❖ Lightly flour both sides of chops. Melt margarine in nonstick skillet over medium heat until foaming. Brown chops quickly on both sides. Remove, reserve pan drippings. Add green onions, garlic, mushrooms and thyme and sauté an additional minute. Return chops to skillet, add beer; bring to a boil. Reduce heat, cover and simmer for 7 to 8 minutes. Season with salt and pepper and garnish with parsley, if desired. Serve 4.

❖ Hint: Buy an entire boneless loin of pork and cut it into serving sizes. Freeze until you're ready to use.

America's Cut™ with Balsamic Vinegar

2 1 1/2-inch thick boneless center-cut pork chops
1 1/2 teaspoons lemon pepper
1/2 teaspoon vegetable oil
2 tablespoons chicken broth
3 tablespoons balsamic vinegar
2 teaspoons butter

❖ Pat chops dry. Coat with lemon pepper. Heat oil in heavy skillet over medium-high heat. Add chops; brown on first side 8 minutes; turn and cook for 7 minutes more. Remove chops from pan and keep warm. Add broth and vinegar to skillet; cook stirring until syrupy (about 1 to 2 minutes). Stir in butter, blend well. Spoon sauce over chops. Serve immediately.

❖ Serve with Orange Ginger Asparagus, Chilled Mushroom Salad and Hot Rolls.

Courtesy of National Pork Producers

Pork with Mushrooms

Serve with hot cooked rice, French-cut green beans, carrot salad.

1 to 2 teaspoons vegetable oil
4 1½-inch boneless loin chops
2 cups sliced fresh mushrooms
¾ cup chicken broth
4 teaspoons cornstarch
¼ teaspoon dried tarragon, crushed
1 1-ounce slice Swiss cheese, torn
1 tablespoon dry white wine

❖ Preheat a browning dish on High (100%) power for 5 minutes. Add oil; swirl to coat. Add pork chops. Cover with lid and microwave on High for 3 minutes. Turn pork chops over; rotate dish a half turn. cover and microwave on High for 3 to 5 minutes more or until done or to 155 to 160° F internal temperature. Cover meat tightly with foil; let stand about 10 minutes while preparing sauce.

❖ Add mushrooms to browning dish. Cover and microwave on High for 2 minutes. Remove dish from oven. In a microwave-safe 2-cup measure combine broth, cornstarch and tarragon. Microwave broth mixture on High for 3 to 4 minutes, stirring twice or until thickened and bubbly. Stir in cheese until melted; stir in wine. Add broth mixture to browning dish with mushrooms. Microwave, uncovered, on High for about 2 minutes or until sauce is heated through. Serve mushroom sauce with pork chops. Serves 4.

Baked Zucchini and Sausage

I like this recipe even better made with eggplant.

2 pounds medium-sized zucchini
1 cup bread crumbs
2 eggs
2 tablespoons water
6 tablespoons oil
1½ pounds sweet or hot Italian sausage
¼ cup margarine
½ cup chopped onion
¼ cup flour
1 13¾-ounce can chicken broth
½ cup half and half cream
½ cup grated Parmesan cheese

❖ Wash zucchini, remove ends. Cut into slices ½ inch thick. Place bread crumbs in shallow dish. Beat eggs and water in small bowl. Dip squash slices in eggs and crumbs. Heat 2 tablespoons oil in large skillet. Brown squash on both sides, adding remaining oil as needed. Remove squash from skillet and set aside. Cook sausages in skillet over low heat for about 20 minutes or until lightly browned, turning frequently.

❖ While sausages brown, melt butter in saucepan over medium heat. Add onion, sauté for 1 minute. Add flour. Remove from heat. Stir in broth gradually. Return pan to heat. Cook until thickened, stirring constantly. Stir in half and half and cheese. Cook until just heated. Preheat oven to 375° F. Lightly grease 13x9x2-inch oval baking dish. Spoon ½ the sauce into dish; arrange half the zucchini in layers in dish. Place sausages in center, arrange remaining zucchini around edge of dish. Spoon remaining sauce over sausages. Cover dish with foil. Bake for 20 minutes or until bubbly. Garnish with parsley.

❖ Slice veal into 4 equal medallions and grill to your preference. In sauté pan, heat olive oil; add shrimp and mushrooms. Toss shrimp and mushrooms once or twice and add sherry. Reduce (cook-off) to half volume of sherry. Now add chicken stock, butter and reduce this sauce until slightly thickened; season to taste with salt, pepper and garlic powder. Place sauce on top of veal medallions—2 per plate. Garnish—fan sliced raw apple with skin. Serve immediately with baked stuffed potatoes, green beans almandine and mixed greens with raspberry vinaigrette.

Stifle

An old English recipe from my Grandmother Sherman, who provides another great recipe for leftovers. Serve with peas and applesauce.

6 potatoes, sliced thin
2 onions, sliced thin
2 cups roast pork, sliced thin or in small pieces (remove fat)
Salt and pepper
Flour
Water
Leftover gravy, if available

❖ In a large saucepan or heavy pot, layer potatoes, onions and roast pork and then season with salt, pepper and dust generously with flour. Repeat this procedure until all ingredients are used. Add gravy, if available, and enough water to fill pot about ¾ full. If you do not have gravy, just use the same amount of water. Cover tightly and cook over medium heat for 25 to 30 minutes or until potatoes are done.

❖ Note: Do not remove cover while cooking.

Land and Sea with Tri Mushrooms

Ever wonder what ever happened to any of your former students? I often do. One of my Senior Family and Consumer Students, David I. Muller, is now a graduate of Rhode Island School of Design, Providence, Rhode Island, and a member of the American Culinary Federation. He is currently employed as Executive Chef of the Norton Country Club in Massachusetts. He fondly called me "Auntie." His original recipe follows and is a "piece de resistance"; he must have had good teachers along the way. All kidding aside, David, we're very proud of you!

14 ounces veal ribeye, trimmed of fat
1½ tablespoons olive oil
4 jumbo shrimp, peeled, split in half
1 cup Tri mushrooms
(2 ounces shiitake mushrooms, cut in half, 2 ounces button mushrooms, cut in half and 2 ounces straw mushrooms)
⅓ cup dry sherry wine
½ cup chicken stock
2 ounces butter
Salt, pepper and garlic powder to taste

Newport Escallopine of Veal

4 thin slices of veal
1 teaspoon butter
1 teaspoon sherry
1/2 lemon

❖ Cut 4 very thin slices of veal. Put in a hot skillet with 1 teaspoon butter and 1 teaspoon sherry. Cook for 5 minutes. Remove from pan and place veal on serving plate. Add more sherry, butter and lemon to pan. Blend well and pour juice over veal.

The Rhode Island Red

Rhode Island Red chickens, probably one of the finest breeds developed in this country, were developed around the mid 1860s. In 1896, Isaac C. Wilbour began to advertise his "Rhode Island Reds" in poultry journals. The first standard was published for the breed in 1898 originating in Little Compton, Rhode Island. American Standards

were adopted as the Standards of Perfection in 1904. Fine red birds with shining greenish-black tail feathers were the look for roosters and the hens were a light buff with lacings of black. The breed today has more a mahogany red in the classic show birds. Outstanding for meat and laying performance, they are still very popular birds. In early years, a monument was dedicated in the village of Adamsville where they were developed. "There are two country stores and a grist mill that still grinds out white flint corn, from farmers thereabouts, into jonnycake meal by Gray's." The Rhode Island General Assembly named "The Rhode Island Red" as the official state bird.

Cashew Chicken

1 pound boneless chicken
1/2 pound snow peas
1/2 pound mushrooms
4 scallions
1/4 cup soy sauce
2 tablespoons cornstarch
1/2 teaspoon sugar
1/4 teaspoon pepper
1 cup chicken broth or 1 cube chicken bouillon and 1 cup water
1/4 cup oil
1 can bamboo shoots, drained
1 4-ounce package cashew nuts

❖ Slice chicken into 1/8-inch thin slices, then cut into 1-inch squares. Arrange on a dish. Remove the ends and strings from fresh snow peas, set aside in cold water. Clean and slice mushrooms. Slice scallions in 1-inch slices using entire scallion except end.

❖ In a bowl, mix soy sauce, cornstarch, sugar and pepper, add to chicken broth, set aside.

❖ In a frying pan, heat 1 tablespoon oil over moderate heat and add cashews all at once, cook for 1 minute stirring constantly as not to burn.

Remove from frying pan, set aside. Add remainder of oil to pan, then chicken. Cook quickly, stirring constantly until chicken is white. Take out chicken, set aside. Add peas and mushrooms, then pour in broth, cover and simmer tor 2 minutes. Add bamboo shoots, stir until sauce is thickened, stirring constantly for another minute, uncovered. Mix in scallions and chicken, sprinkle with nuts. Serve immediately.

Chicken Rumford

Serve with a green salad and, for dessert, baked apples, apple crisp or even a grapenut custard.

4 boneless chicken breasts (about 1 to 1½ pounds)
2 tablespoons margarine or oil
1 small onion, sliced
1 large carrot, sliced
4 large potatoes, peeled and sliced
½ cup fresh sliced mushrooms or 1 3-ounce can mushrooms
Bay leaf
Salt and pepper to taste
2 cups stock

❖ Cut chicken into pieces convenient for serving. Heat margarine or oil in a large frying pan. Add chicken and cook until golden brown on 1 side, then turn, add onion and carrot. Brown second side of chicken.

❖ Have ready sliced potatoes and mushrooms. Arrange all ingredients in layers in a 2-quart baking dish. Add bay leaf, seasonings and stock. Note: If not stock is available, use 1 chicken bouillon cube and 2 cups water. Bake, covered, for about 2 hours in a slow oven 325° F. Serves 4.

Easy Chicken Pie

Serve with green salad and cranberry relish.

1 cup frozen peas
1 cup cooked carrots or 1 package frozen peas and carrots
2 cups cooked chicken or turkey
1 10½-ounce can cream of chicken soup
1 can of water
Biscuit Topping

❖ Microwave in a 2-quart covered casserole for 5 minutes on High.

❖ Drop Biscuit Topping on top of hot chicken mixture by tablespoonfuls. Bake, uncovered, in a preheated 400° F oven for 15 to 20 minutes or until biscuits are cooked. Makes 3 to 4 servings.

Biscuit Topping

2 cups flour
1 tablespoon baking powder
½ teaspoon salt
7 tablespoons shortening
1 cup milk

❖ Sift together flour, baking powder and salt. Cut shortening in with a pastry blender or 2 knives until mixture looks like cornmeal. Using a fork, lightly mix in milk until mixture is just moistened.

Chicken Supreme Sandwich

8 generous slices chicken or turkey
4 slices of toast
2 cups chicken base, cream sauce or soup with 1/4 cup milk
1 10 1/2-ounce can cream of chicken
8 slices sharp Cheddar cheese
8 slices crisp bacon

❖ Place chicken slices on hot buttered toast, top with cream sauce and cheese slices.

❖ Place under hot broiler just long enough to melt cheese.

❖ Top each open-faced sandwich with 2 slices of crisp bacon. Serves 4.

Joc's Chicken

1 egg, beaten
1/4 to 1/2 cup orange juice
4 large boneless chicken breasts
1/2 cup crushed cornflakes
1/2 cup chopped coconut
1/2 to 1 teaspoon curry powder
1/4 cup margarine, melted

❖ Make a marinade of the egg and orange juice and cover chicken with it for about 1/2 to 1 hour.

❖ Mix together cornflakes, coconut, and curry powder. Dip marinated chicken in cornflake mixture and put in a shallow baking dish, then pour melted margarine over top.

❖ I sometimes add a little more orange juice to prevent chicken from drying out.

❖ Cover with foil. Bake at 350° F for 20 to 30 minutes, depending on how thick the chicken is.

❖ Remove foil the last 5 minutes to make it a little crispy on the outside.

Marion's Heart Healthy Chicken

If you are using a cast-iron frying pan or one that will go directly into the oven, you don't need to use baking dish. Serve with baked potato and a green vegetable of course!

1 1/2 pounds boneless chicken or 6 boned chicken breasts
1/4 cup flour
1/4 teaspoon salt, optional
1/8 teaspoon pepper
1/2 teaspoon rosemary or summer savory
1/4 cup egg substitute or 2 egg whites
1/4 teaspoon turmeric
1/2 teaspoon cinnamon
Dried bread crumbs
Oil, as little as possible

❖ Trim any skin or fat from chicken. On a piece of waxed paper or a flat plate, mix flour, salt, pepper and rosemary. Beat egg white or egg substitute in a soup plate with turmeric and cinnamon and last but not least, put dried bread crumbs on another piece of waxed paper a little at a time. Here's what to do...dip chicken pieces in flour mixture, then egg mixture and coat with bread crumbs. In a large frying pan heat oil and brown chicken on both sides, then remove to baking pan and bake in 350° F oven for 30 minutes. May be served in same dish or a sauce can be made by adding 1/2 cup white wine or chicken broth to baking dish, heating thoroughly. Serve immediately.

Nut and Honey Chicken

3 pounds chicken (pieces or boneless)
4 tablespoons margarine or oil
1/3 cup cornflake crumbs
1/2 cup chopped nuts
1/8 teaspoon garlic powder
1/4 cup mustard
1/2 cup honey
1/2 teaspoon salt, optional
1/8 teaspoon pepper
Parsley for garnish

❖ Wash and dry chicken (skins may be removed). Melt margarine in a shallow baking pan. Set aside. In another shallow dish combine cornflake crumbs, chopped nuts, and garlic powder. Dip prepared chicken in melted margarine, then coat with cornflake mixture. Put all chicken in bottom of shallow baking pan in a single layer. Mix together mustard, honey, salt and pepper. Pour over chicken. Bake in a 375° F oven for 30 minutes. Bake until chicken is tender and not pink. Garnish with parsley and serve immediately.

Stuffed Chicken Breasts with Orange

Great for buffet or large party...I used it many times for both...In 1976, my high school home economics class served the Bicentennial Band and participants, 125 persons, with no trouble at all. Goes well with sliced minted carrots, green beans or broccoli and, of course, some kind of cranberry sauce or relish.

6 large boneless chicken breasts
   (about 1½ to 2 pounds)
1 cup uncooked rice
1 medium onion, finely chopped
2 cups Pepperidge Farm stuffing mix
   or your choice
1 cup orange juice
1 teaspoon poultry seasoning
1/2 teaspoon salt
1/4 teaspoon pepper
1/4 pound margarine
Toothpicks
1 orange
2 cups orange juice

❖ Chill chicken breasts in freezer about ½ hour before preparing them. They will handle better if a little icy. Slice and flatten each chick-

en breast with a very sharp knife. Remove any fat or skin.

❖ In a large bowl, mix rice, onion, stuffing mix, 1 cup orange juice, poultry seasoning, salt and pepper. Mix well. Dice margarine into small dots and place 1 on each piece of prepared chicken. Place a handful of stuffing in the center of each (about 3 tablespoons). Fold up sides of chicken and roll in other direction like a jelly roll. Secure with toothpick. Place tucked side down in the bottom of a 2 to 3-quart baking dish or pan. Thinly slice orange in rounds. Cut in half only to the rind on 1 side. Twist to a figure 8 and place on top of rolled chicken. Pour remaining orange juice over chicken. Cover with foil. Refrigerate until ready to bake.

❖ Can be prepared the night before or in the morning. If having for supper, bake in 350° F oven for 35 to 40 minutes, removing foil for last 5 minutes. Check to see if chicken is white and flakes. Serve immediately.

King's Quail with Wild Rice and Mushrooms

This is really a gourmet one-dish meal, fit for a King! Serve with a green salad and, of course, a white wine.

2 quail or Cornish game hens
1½ cups white wine
Pinch of basil
Pinch of summer savory
Salt and pepper
2 shallots, minced
1 cup sliced mushrooms
1 cup uncooked wild rice
4 tablespoons olive oil
2 cups chicken stock or broth

❖ Wash and cut quail in half lengthwise. Marinate quail or Cornish hen in marinade made from wine, basil, summer savory, salt and pepper for 1 to 2 hours, turning occasionally. Remove and pat dry. (Save and strain marinade.) In a frying pan, sauté shallots, mushrooms and wild rice in olive oil. Spread rice mixture in a large rectangular baking dish. Put split birds cavity side down on top of rice mixture. Bring marinade to a boil and add chicken stock. Pour over rice and birds. Roast,

uncovered, at 400° F, basting frequently. Test for doneness in meaty part of bird. Serves 4.

Fettucine Alfredo with Blue Cheese

1 pound wide egg noodles
5 ounces blue cheese
½ cup butter
2 cups heavy cream
¼ teaspoon salt
¼ teaspoon pepper
2 eggs, slightly beaten
¼ cup finely chopped parsley

❖ Prepare noodles according to package directions. Drain. Place in large serving bowl. In medium saucepan, combine 4 ounces cheese, butter, cream, salt and pepper. Cook over low heat, stirring constantly until cheese and butter are melted. Remove from heat. Stir ½ cup of mixture into eggs and mix well. Return mixture to pan and cook for 1 minute longer or until slightly thickened. Toss with hot noodles. Sprinkle with remaining crumbled cheese and chopped parsley. Serve immediately.

Cavetelli with Broccoli

1 pound frozen or fresh cavetelli, stuffed
½ cup olive oil
2 tablespoons butter
1 to 2 cloves garlic
1 10½-ounce package frozen chopped broccoli or florets
Salt and pepper
Grated Parmesan cheese

❖ Cook cavetelli in 5 to 6 quarts salted boiling water. In a saucepan, heat olive oil and butter, add garlic and sauté just until brown. (Do not burn.) Discard garlic.

❖ Cook broccoli according to package directions or until barely tender. When pasta is done, drain and empty into a large bowl that has been heated by putting very hot water in it and letting it stand for a few minutes. (Don't forget to pour the water out.) Toss pasta with olive oil, cooked broccoli, salt and pepper to taste. Sprinkle generously with freshly grated Parmesan cheese. Serve immediately. Serves 4 to 6.

Pasta Salad

As some of you "real Rhode Islanders" remember, until recent years, we had only heard of Macaroni Salad—only made if you had "leftover macaroni" not a "special recipe." Well, as everything seems to change and evolve we discovered that the lowly leftover dish of many years had now come to us from the West Coast as "Pasta Salad" or even as "cold pasta primavera." Well, here's a favorite to share with you from a friend of a friend's recipe. I'm not sure if it's a macaroni or a pasta salad or a leftover, a planned over or planned that way...well you know how things are. Makes a good-sized bowl that will disappear quickly at a picnic or large gathering or will last several meals for a small family.

Unbelievable Lasagna

4 to 5 cups spaghetti sauce
8 ounces lasagna noodles
1 pound ricotta or cottage cheese
8 ounces mozzarella cheese, grated
1 cup grated Parmesan cheese

❖ In a 9x13-inch baking pan, spread 1 cup of sauce; arrange a layer of un-cooked noodles topped with sauce, ricotta, mozzarella and Parmesan cheeses and sauce, repeat and end with a layer of noodles; pour on remaining sauce, top with mozzarella and Parmesan cheeses. Bake at 350° F for 1½ hours or until light brown. Let stand for 15 minutes. Cut into squares. Makes 6 to 8 servings.

Masi's Manicotti

One of the easiest pastas to make. Kathi used this one when teaching home economics and the kids loved doing it.

2 cups flour
1/4 teaspoon salt
1 cup water
2 eggs
Margarine

❖ Mix flour, salt, water and eggs until smooth. Melt ¼ teaspoon margarine in a 6-inch skillet. Add about ¼ cup batter and roll liquid in pan, so entire bottom of pan is covered; cook until just firm. Do not brown. Turn, let cook only 10 to 20 seconds on other side. Cook much the same as crêpes. Set aside to cool on a cookie sheet. Repeat with remaining batter. Fill and roll like a jelly roll, but be sure and turn in ends first. Lay side by side in a buttered 9x13-inch baking dish. Cover with tomato sauce of your choice. Bake at 350° F for 30 to 40 minutes.

Spinach Filling:
1   10½-ounce package frozen chopped spinach
½ pound freshly grated mozzarella cheese
2 cups ricotta cheese
1 egg, beaten
1/2 cup Parmesan cheese
1 tablespoon chopped parsley
1/4 teaspoon nutmeg
Salt and pepper

❖ Thaw and drain spinach. Place all ingredients in bowl; mix well. Place about 1 tablespoon filling on each shell and roll to enclose.

Fran's Pasta Salad

An excellent choice for a buffet or family meal

1/2 pound pasta
1/4 cup corn or olive oil
2 cups broccoli, use a whole head with florets
1/4 cup sliced scallions
1 clove garlic, peeled
2 teaspoons fresh basil
1 teaspoon salt
1 cup chopped cherry tomatoes
1/2 cup grated Parmesan cheese
Fresh parsley

❖ Cook pasta according to package directions. Meanwhile, heat oil in a large skillet and add broccoli florets, scallions, garlic, basil and salt. Toss and stir-fry until broccoli is *al dente*, about 4 minutes.

❖ Add drained pasta, tomatoes, and cheese, toss lightly. Put in a large bowl and cover with plastic wrap. Chill until serving time. Garnish with fresh parsley.

❖ Serve in bowl or on a bed of lettuce.

❖ Variation: For a main dish salad, add 1½ cups cooked diced ham, cooked shrimp or 1 can of tuna, drained. For extra color and flavor, add chopped black olives and diced green pepper.

Peg's Cottage Cheese-Bacon Quiche

1 9-inch unbaked pastry shell
4 eggs
2 cups cottage cheese
1 teaspoon salt
1/8 teaspoon white pepper
Dash of nutmeg
6 slices bacon, cooked, drained, crumbled

❖ Preheat oven to 425° F.

❖ Prick pastry shell and bake for 10 minutes, cool.

❖ Reduce oven to 350° F. In bowl, beat eggs until well mixed. Add rest of ingredients. Pour mixture into center of shell.

❖ Bake for 45 minutes or until knife inserted in center comes out clean. Let stand for 10 minutes.

Spinach Quiche

This mixture could also be used in miniature pastry shells, using 1 recipe for a double crust. Makes about 2 dozen small appetizers.

1 pound spinach, cooked, drained
2 cups light cream
1/3 cup grated Swiss cheese
4 eggs
1/2 teaspoon nutmeg
Salt and pepper to taste
1 9-inch pastry shell, uncooked

❖ Chop spinach into very small pieces. Beat together cream, cheeses, eggs, nutmeg, salt and pepper very thoroughly.

❖ Layer spinach in the bottom of the unbaked pastry shell and then pour egg mixture over spinach.

❖ Bake in preheated 350° F oven for 25 to 30 minutes or until a knife inserted in the center comes out clean. Serve hot.

"The Clambake" and Other Tales of the Sea

Rhode Island Clambakes

According to the American Indian Federation, in the mid 1500s "natives moved to the seashore, in summer, built wigwams and covered them with grass mats. Their main food was shellfish. They wrapped the shellfish in seaweed and baked it over the hot coals. So this was the beginning of the Rhode Island Clambakes."

Indian-Style Clambake

A modern Indian version for a Rhode Island Clambake for 24 people.

3/4 bushel of steamer clams
24 white potatoes
24 sweet potatoes
4 dozen ears of sweet corn
6 pounds fish filets
48 link pork sausage
24 lobsters
3 pounds onions
4 cans brown bread
2 1/2 pounds butter

❖ Clean clams by soaking in salted water and rinsing to free them of sand. Scrub both white and sweet potatoes (leave skins on). Husk corn, with exception of inner layer and remove corn silks. Pull inner husks up to protect corn. Wrap fish around 2 sausage and wrap individually in cheesecloth. Put steamers in rack. We have wooden racks, 30 inches square and 4 inches deep with wire mesh bottoms. Everything is put separately in these containers.

❖ Pack in this order, on white hot stones, covered with Rock weed. Fire is started about an hour before, to heat stones in a shallow 48-inch pit. When ready to pack, follow this order: clams, potatoes, onions, fish and sausage, lobster and corn. Cover with a clean sheet, and cover everything with a canvas. Let steam for 45 minutes. Serve with brown bread and drawn butter.

❖ Note: The way to really learn how to do a clambake is to take advantage of the University of Rhode Island's programs given at the Sea Grant College each year. For information, contact: University of Rhode Island, Kingston, Rhode Island 02881.

Bucket Bakes

Since a genuine clambake is an art in itself, I have provided recipes for what is called "A Bucket Bake" or a Kettle Bake, a Clam Boil or whatever. Any of these recipes will provide you with the "feeling of being at the seashore on a summer's day." There are several good books available on the subject as well.

At a "real" bake, little necks on the half shell, chowder and clamcakes are generally served while the bakemaster tends the steaming bake. Then the bake is served very hot. Watermelon for dessert and maybe Indian pudding, blueberry or apple pie and vanilla ice cream.

Another version is called "The Shore Dinner" starting off with steaming bowls of Rhode Island Red Chowder and clamcakes, then lobster, corn and coleslaw finished up with all the watermelon you can eat. Rocky Point probably is still the most famous for these. In the late 1800s, the "trollies" would go on weekends for special excursions for a day at the shore and of course "a Shore Dinner."

Virginia's Kettle Bake

The following recipe is based on serving 4 healthy appetites.

8 medium onions
4 quarts clams
1½ pounds link sausage
1½ pounds fish filets (cod/haddock)
8 ears corn
4 small sweet potatoes
4 small white potatoes

❖ Parboil onions for about 15 minutes.

❖ Scrub clams and place in large kettle. Next sausage links. Cut fish into 4 portions and place individually into paper bags (may use ordinary brown paper bags). Place on top of sausage.

❖ Now for the onions, corn, sweet potatoes and very last white potatoes which do not have to be put into bags. Pour 2 to 3 cups of water into kettle and cover tightly.

❖ When potatoes are tender all is done! Time about ½ to ¾ of an hour. Paper bags should be removed before serving.

❖ The sausage flavors the vegetables nicely and the broth is delicious!

Adapted from
Echoes from South County Kitchens

Clam Boil

Salty's favorite from the Providence Gas Company

8 pounds white potatoes
8 pounds sweet potatoes
7½ broiler halves
Salt and pepper to taste
1½ pounds butter
2½ dozen ears corn
15 lobsters
1 bushel clams
Mayonnaise if lobster is served cold
3 dozen rolls
½ pound coffee
1½ pints cream
1 large watermelon

❖ Use large wash boiler set on cement bricks or rocks and build fire between rocks.

❖ Place white and sweet potatoes on bottom of boiler and lay chicken on top. Dot with salt, pepper and but-

ter. Add 2 inches of water to boiler and allow to steam 30 to 45 minutes depending on the size of potatoes and chickens.

❖ Add corn which has been husked and tied loosely in cheesecloth; on top of this place the lobsters and then the clams which also have been tied loosely in cheesecloth. Add more water to make 2 inches in the bottom of the boiler.

❖ Cover and steam about 30 minutes longer or until clams open. If the kettle stops steaming, add more water.

❖ If white fish is added, tie about 2 or 3 servings in each cheesecloth and put on top of corn. Then continue. Serves 30.

❖ Serve with mayonnaise, rolls, coffee and cream, and, of course, watermelon for dessert.

Robin's Brenton Cove Clambake

3 pints water or seawater
Seaweed, celery or lettuce leaves
6 pieces chicken, broiler
6 small potatoes
1 link sausage
1 medium-sized onion
6 ears corn
4 dozen small steamer clams
6 1-pound live lobsters
1 medium-sized potatoes

❖ In the bottom of a clam steamer, pour 3 pints water (sea water, if on a boat).

❖ Cover steamer with upper section of the pot, and pack in the following order:

❖ Generously layer wet seaweed or wet celery or lettuce leaves. In a brown sandwich bag wrap chicken, 6 small potatoes, sausage and onion, then put on top of seaweed.

❖ Husk corn, removing silk but leaving husk intact and layer.

❖ Wash and put clams in a cheese-cloth bag, then lobsters, more seaweed and in the center put

1 medium-sized potato. Cover the pot tightly. The potato is the thermometer—the clambake is done when the potato is.

❖ Cook for about 2 hours; when done bake has steamed through. Serves 6.

Adapted from Edward King House,
Newport, Rhode Island

John's Best Steamers (Clams)

4 pounds clams (steamers)
12 ounces beer
2 to 3 inches of dried pepperoni, finely diced

❖ Be sure and have really fresh clams. Soak in a large pan, covered with cold water, and add about 1/4 cup of cornmeal. Let soak for about half an hour...Drain and rinse clams thoroughly about 3 times. (Believe it or not the cornmeal is the best way to get those clams to spit out the sand.)

Serve in a large bowl, with a cup of broth on the side and Rhode Island Italian Bread sliced thick...This amount will serve 2 hungry people...but 3 to 4 if for an appetizer. Enjoy....

❖ Put drained clams in the bottom of a large pot. Add beer and pepperoni. Cover. Bring to a boil and steam for 10 to 15 minutes or until clams open.

Clambake Casserole

1 10½-ounce can mushroom soup
1 6½-ounce can minced clams
35 Ritz crackers

❖ Butter a 1½-quart casserole dish. Mix together soup, clams and juice, and crumbled crackers. Reserve 1/4 cup of crumbs for the top. Bake at 350° F for 20 to 25 minutes.

Clam Cake Safaris

There probably are as many recipes for clam cakes as there are for chowder...Many a day families have gone on a search of "the best clam cake." "My mother and grandmother made this safari on many a Tuesday afternoon and still thought Crescent Park was the best!

Clam Cakes

Here are a few for you to try. Hint: Don't make too big or they will be raw in the middle.

1½ cups flour
1½ teaspoons baking powder
½ teaspoon salt
¼ teaspoon pepper
1 egg, beaten
2 6½-ounce cans minced clams
Milk

❖ Sift dry ingredients into egg. Lightly stir in clams and juice. Add only enough milk to moisten, so batter may be dropped by tablespoonfuls into hot deep fat. Turn, using a metal slotted spoon. Drain on paper towels.

❖ Note: To clarify fat, put in a raw sliced potato when done with frying and strain into a clean container.

Quahog Cakes

(Old Yankee recipe from Sonia's great-grandmother)

2 6-ounce cans minced clams or ½ cup fresh ground quahogs
4 eggs, beaten
1 onion, grated
½ teaspoon salt
Dash of pepper
10 to 15 saltines, crumbled

❖ In a bowl, mix together minced clams, beaten eggs, onion, salt and pepper. Stir crumbled saltines into clam mixture and let stand for 10 to 15 minutes until crackers are absorbed in mixture. Spoon into hot frying pan with oil. Cook until brown and turn. Brown other side. Serve immediately

❖ Leftover mashed potatoes can be substituted for the crackers. Add enough mashed potatoes until mixture can be dropped by spoonfuls into hot fat.

Stuffed Quahogs–Baked then Broiled

Not the usual, but delicious

1 cup stale bread crumbs
Dash of onion powder
2 cups ground raw quahogs and juice
Salt and pepper
½ teaspoon poultry seasoning
Shredded Cheddar cheese
2 or 3 strips bacon

❖ Combine bread crumbs, onion powder, quahogs and juice, salt, pepper and poultry seasoning and spoon into twelve 3-inch quahog shells. Place on foil-lined baking sheet.

❖ Top with shredded Cheddar cheese and 2 or 3 strips raw bacon.

❖ Bake at 400° F for 15 minutes, then broil until the bacon is crisp. Serves 4.

Barbara's Modern Codfish Cakes

Old fashioned style, but real easy now!

1 pound dried codfish
Instant mashed potatoes
(I like Idaho best)
Milk
Pepper
¼ cup egg substitute
Flour

❖ Soak dried codfish to freshen in cold water for about ½ hour before cooking, changing water several times. Simmer codfish in a heavy saucepan, cover with water and simmer for 20 minutes or until tender. If making creamed codfish, save broth for cream sauce. Now comes the easy part. Using the directions on the instant potatoes for 8 to 10 servings, follow package directions except reduce liquid by ¾ of a cup. When potato is ready, beat in flaked codfish, add egg and beat until fully mixed. Patties may be shaped for frying by using an ice cream scoop to measure mixture.

Put scoop of fish mixture on waxed paper covered with flour. Shape into a patty 1 inch thick. Cook in a frying pan with a little shortening until well browned on both sides. Will keep several days in refrigerator, or freeze before cooking for one month. Serve with baked beans. Makes 1½ dozen.

❖ I sometimes make miniature patties for appetizers.

Coquilles Saint Jacques

1 cup flour
2 cups milk
10 tablespoons butter
1 cup bread crumbs
1 cup chopped onions
2 cloves garlic, chopped
1 pound cape or sea scallops, chopped
1 pound fresh mushrooms, chopped
½ cup dry vermouth (or dry white wine)
½ cup grated Parmesan cheese
Pinch of saffron
1 teaspoon salt
Pinch of cayenne pepper
½ teaspoon black pepper
Scallop or quahog shells for filling

❖ Combine flour and milk, blend and set aside.

❖ Melt 2 tablespoons of butter; mix with bread crumbs. Melt 1 stick butter (8 tablespoons) in a thick saucepan. Do not brown. Add onions; sauté for 2 minutes, stirring. Add garlic; cook for 1 minute. Add scallops; cook for 2 minutes, stirring; add chopped mushrooms. Bring to a boil; cook for 2 minutes then add wine, cheese, saffron and blended mixture of milk and flour.

❖ Cook for about 5 to 8 minutes. Mixture should thicken. Add salt, cayenne and black pepper. Let cool in refrigerator before placing in shells. Spoon into shells and cover each with 1 tablespoon of buttered bread crumbs.

❖ Bake in moderate 350° F oven for 20 to 30 minutes or until they bubble.

Courtesy of the Chief

Island Deviled Crab

I like to serve this with baby new potatoes and a garnish of whole string beans, sliced carrots and sliced zucchini.

1   11-ounce can crab meat
4 slices bread, crumbled
¼ cup butter, melted
1 tablespoon Worcestershire sauce
2 teaspoons lemon juice
1 tablespoon minced onion or shallots
⅛ teaspoon salt
⅛ teaspoon cayenne pepper
Milk to moisten
Buttered crumbs for topping

❖ Combine crab meat, crumbled bread, melted butter, Worcestershire sauce, lemon juice, onion or shallots, salt and cayenne pepper; mix well. If bread crumbs do not stick to each other, add milk a little at a time until bread crumbs absorb milk. The mixture should be rather soft. Pack loosely into a shallow baking dish, individual ramekins or thoroughly scrubbed scallop, crab or lobster shells. Top with buttered bread crumbs made by crumbling 2 more slices of bread and moistened with 2 tablespoons melted butter.

The Secret of Good Bluefish

Bluefish and zucchini seem to be something the Islands all seem to have in abundance. A friend of mine who used to be a fish and game warden said, "The real secret is to get it fresh and dressed as quickly as possible or it will taste like crankcase oil." Well, it's not that bad...but handling of all fish—keeping it chilled and using it right away—is one of the secrets.

Baked Bluefish

My grandmother used to cook mackerel this way, which helps to take the oil out of fish.

❖ Line a baking pan with brown paper. Lay bluefish filets on paper. Cover with sliced onion, pepper and salt. Bake at 350° F for ½ to ¾ of an hour or until fish flakes.

Bake at 350° F until delicately brown and very hot...about 15 to 20 minutes. Garnish with slices of lemon and a sprig or parsley.

Broiled Bluefish

1 large onion, finely chopped
1 green pepper, finely chopped
1 bluefish filet
Enough mayonnaise to cover filet

❖ Mix onion, green pepper and mayonnaise. Place fish on greased foil on a broiler pan. Cover with mayonnaise and broil 4 inches from heat. Cook for 10 to 12 minutes or until fish flakes.

❖ Note: If fish is very large, bake in a 350° F oven until almost done, then broil until brown.

Shaw's Haddock Delmonico

2 tablespoons margarine
2 tablespoons flour
1 teaspoon dry mustard
1/8 teaspoon pepper
1/4 cup minced onion
1/4 teaspoon salt
1 cup milk
1/2 cup Cheddar cheese
2 pounds haddock

❖ Make a white sauce by melting margarine; stir in flour. Cook for several minutes, then add mustard, pepper, onion, salt and milk. Continue stirring until mixture begins to thicken and there are no lumps. Add cheese and continue cooking until cheese is melted. Layer fish in a flat buttered baking dish. Top with sauce. Bake at 350° F for 30 minutes.

Home-Fried Fish

1 to 1 1/2 pounds white filets, scrod, haddock, sole, cod
1 egg, beaten
2 to 3 tablespoons milk
Cornflake crumbs

❖ Wash and dry fish, cut into 6 pieces. Place in dish. Cover with lemon juice, soak for at least 1/2 hour. Dis-

card juice. Pour butter over fish, sprinkle with black pepper. Broil for 10 minutes and baste with seasonings. Set aside to cool. (May be prepared early in the day).

❖ Cut fish into serving size. Dip in egg wash of egg and milk. Coat with crushed cornflakes on both sides. Fry in a thin layer of hot corn oil in a skillet until brown on both sides. Or put in a metal fish platter which has just a little oil on bottom and bake at 350° F until coating is brown and fish is flaky.

❖ Note: May use an egg substitute for egg wash.

Polynesian Fish

A recipe for 2 cups medium white sauce and a small can shrimp can be used instead of shrimp soup.

3 pound halibut, swordfish, or cod steak
1/3 cup lemon juice
1/4 cup melted margarine
1/4 teaspoon black pepper
1   10-ounce can shrimp soup
1/2 cup sour cream
1 tablespoon cut chives
1/2 cup tiny shrimp, optional

❖ Mix soup with sour cream and spoon onto top of each piece of fish. Bake at 325° F for 30 minutes. Serve in baking dish garnished with chives and tiny shrimp. Serve with tomato juice, hard rolls or toast points, tossed salad, green peas, fresh fruit cups. Serves 6.

Lobster Cocktail

Here's an easy recipe and you can figure out how much you need for your crowd of 1 or 10.

❖ For each serving allow 1/4 cup lobster meat, cut in pieces. Blend with 2 tablespoons tomato catsup, 2 tablespoons sherry, optional, 1 teaspoon lemon juice and 4 drops Tabasco sauce. Chill thoroughly and serve in cocktail glasses

❖ You have the choice of boiling your own lobster, buying the meat from the fish market or, if in desperation, use frozen or canned meat.

Lobster Salad

❖ As far as I'm concerned there's only one way to make lobster salad and that's just with mayo...For each cup of boiled and chilled lobster meat cut into small pieces, allow 1 tablespoon of mayonnaise. Mix thoroughly and chill again. Place on crisp lettuce leaves and sprinkle with paprika or you can top with a whole lobster claw removed from the shell. Add a side dish of mayonnaise if desired...and if you'd rather, grill a nice roll in butter, add a generous scoop of salad and you've got yourself the best lobster roll.

Tangy Lobster

Great with a fruit salad and cinnamon rolls for a delicious lunch

1/3 cup butter
1 teaspoon Worcestershire sauce
1 tablespoon lemon juice
1 teaspoon dry mustard
1/2 teaspoon salt and pepper
   to taste
2 cups lobster meat

❖ Place all ingredients, except lobster in top part of double boiler. Cook over hot water; stir to blend well. Cut lobster into small pieces; add to mixture and cook for 5 to 6 minutes. Modern Method—Microwave on High only about 2 minutes. Serve on toast with lemon wedges. Serves 4.

Steamed Mussels in Wine Sauce

❖ Place mussels in large kettle. Add 1 1/2 inches white wine. Cover mussels with slices of onion and orange peel.

❖ Steam for about 3 minute or until shells open.

❖ Make white sauce using wine in kettle as base.

2 tablespoons flour
2 tablespoons margarine
   1 cup wine base

❖ Sprinkle chopped chives and parsley over sauce. Arrange mussels on platter. Pour small amount of sauce over each mussel and serve.

Fried Oysters

1 1/2 pints oysters
2 eggs
4 tablespoons milk
4 tablespoons flour
1/2 teaspoon salt
1/4 teaspoon pepper

❖ Drain the oysters. Beat eggs well. Add the milk and beat again.

❖ Dip each oyster in the egg mixture, then coat each slightly with seasoned flour.

❖ Fry in deep fat at 375° F for about 2 1/2 minutes, until crisp. Serves 4 to 6.

Scalloped Oysters

2 cups butter cracker crumbs, crushed
1 pint oysters
Nutmeg
Salt and pepper
1/2 to 1 cup all-purpose cream
4 tablespoons butter

❖ Butter a shallow casserole. Spread with a layer of crumbs. Top with a layer of oysters. Add a dash of nutmeg, salt and pepper and a dribble of cream. Top with another layer of crumbs, oysters, salt, pepper, nutmeg and cream. Sauté remaining crumbs in butter. Cover casserole. Bake at 375° F for 20 minutes.

Salmon Romanoff

1/2 cup finely chopped scallions
2 tablespoons margarine
1 cup cottage cheese
2 cups sour cream
5 dashes of Tabasco sauce
1 1-pound can salmon, red or pink
6 ounces medium noodles, cooked
1 cup shredded Cheddar cheese

❖ Sauté scallions in margarine until transparent. Place in large mixing bowl and stir in cottage cheese, sour cream and Tabasco sauce. Stir in the liquid from can of salmon. Flake and remove bones and skin from salmon. Add to first mixture. Mix lightly. Add cooked noodles; stir into salmon mixture. Turn into well greased casserole, sprinkle with cheese. Bake in preheated 325° F oven for 30 minutes or until cheese is melted and lightly browned. Serves 6.

Block Island Swordfish

The very best when fresh caught or harpooned! One night while walking on the docks in Nantucket, we heard a hugh splash near us. A sports fisherman had landed a very large swordfish and it was being hoisted by chains at the weighing dock. Well, that's the story of the fish that got away. Divers were sent down to retrieve this "catch of the day." Sorry, but we don't remember how many pounds he was—so much for this fish story.

The plainer the better is the way we like it; either broiled on your outside grill or broiled in your range.

❖ Method 1: Select a firm fresh piece of swordfish steak about 1½ inches thick (4 to 6 ounces per serving), rinse and wipe dry. Salt and pepper on both sides. Brush with butter and put on grill or broiler rack. Add more butter to top; sprinkle with lemon juice.

❖ Cook at medium setting, turning carefully in about 8 minutes or so. Butter and sprinkle more lemon juice on side that has been broiled to a nice brown. Continue cooking until fish steak feels firm to the touch and can be flaked lightly with fork. Serve on a hot platter garnished with parsley and lemon wedges. Serve immediately.

❖ Method 2: Many like this quick easy way. Place swordfish steak on rack. Spread your favorite mayonnaise on top of fish. Broil until golden brown, turning carefully. Spread mayonnaise on second side and complete cooking.

❖ Same methods can be used for halibut steaks.

Finnan Haddie

I love this dish, but my biggest disappointment of Finnan Haddie was in Lunenburg, Nova Scotia. I ordered the specialty of the house—but lo and behold, no white sauce or even potato of any kind. It was just poached and served with pickled beets (but it was still tasty).

Finnan Haddie is generally smoked haddock, but with the scarcity of haddock these days you may find cod or other white fish used. If you don't find it in your local fish market, check your yellow pages to find out who does their own smoking. Wallis Seafood in Barrington, Rhode Island, does some, but you must call ahead and order.

Murder Mystery Finnan Haddie

My two favorite ways of serving are a piece of fish covered with sauce, boiled potatoes, peas and yes—pickled beets. The other: take individual baking dishes, put fish in first and put whipped potatoes around the entire edge. Top fish with sauce, sprinkle grated

cheese of any kind over potato and sauce. Put under broiler just until hot and bubbly. We served this for an English Murder Mystery Dinner we hosted with new spring peas, strawberries and cream, Boodles, Bass Ale and lemonade. A delightful time was had by all and no, I won't tell you who was murdered or who the villain was.

1½ to 2 pounds smoked finnan
    haddie
4 tablespoons butter
4 tablespoons flour
2 cups fish broth
2 cups evaporated milk
Pepper to taste

❖ To poach: Put fish in a deep skillet and cover with water. Simmer until fish starts to flake with a fork, about 10 minutes (depends on how thick it is). Remove fish from broth. Remove bones. Set aside 2 cups of the broth.

❖ Make a roux by melting butter and then stirring flour into it. Cook for 4 to 5 minutes, then gradually stir in 2 cups fish broth and evaporated milk. Stir until smooth and thickened. (Some cooks like to add 1 or 2 well-beaten eggs; add a little sauce

to egg before stirring in to insure a smooth sauce.) Add pepper if desired.

"Chief's" Shrimp Scampi

2 pounds peeled and deveined
    shrimp, any size
1 tablespoon olive oil
¼ teaspoon salt
1 tablespoon granulated garlic
Pinch of cayenne pepper
½ teaspoon black pepper
6 tablespoons butter
1 or 2 shallots or scallions, chopped
3 cloves garlic, chopped
1 cup chablis
½ cup vermouth
¼ cup lemon juice
1 cup finely chopped Italian parsley

❖ Thaw shrimp and pat dry. Slit backs of shrimp. Place shrimp in a bowl, add oil, salt, 1 tablespoon garlic, cayenne and black pepper. Toss, let stand for 15 minutes. Heat butter in skillet. (Don't burn.) Add chopped shallots; cook for 45 seconds. Add garlic; cook for 45 seconds. Sauté shrimp 1 or 2 minutes, stirring. Add wine mixture, lemon juice and parsley. Check color; when shrimp is pink, you're home.

Sole Florentine

1 pound filet of sole
1 bay leaf
2 teaspoons lemon juice
2 peppercorns
Water
1 12-ounce package fresh spinach or
    1 10½-ounce package frozen
    chopped spinach
4 tablespoons butter
4 tablespoons flour
1 cup fish stock
1 cup milk or
    cream
Freshly ground nutmeg

❖ In a skillet, put sole, bay leaf, lemon juice, 2 peppercorns; cover fish with water. Simmer for about 8 to 10 minutes. Save liquid and set aside. Steam spinach or cook frozen spinach for 3 minutes. Drain and chop. Make sauce by making a roux and add fish stock and milk. Stir until thickened and no lumps. In a large baking dish or individual ones, put layer of spinach, then fish; top with sauce and sprinkle with ground nutmeg. Bake at 350° F for

about 12 to 15 minutes or until fish flakes and sauce is hot and bubbly. Some like a sprinkling of grated cheese on top the last 5 minutes.

USDA Purchasing and Storing Guidelines for Seafood

The following are suggestions for helping you be a wise shopper when buying seafood: from Martha Smith Patnoad, MS, CHE Consumer Education/Food Safety Extension Specialist of the University of Rhode Island.

According to Patnoad all fish and shellfish are highly perishable products that can spoil or lose quality at any point from harvest to consumption. This indicates that some basic knowledge of purchasing and care of this product is needed to be sure of your diners' well being. First, purchase seafood from a reputable source. Use your nose to determine freshness. It should not have a "fishy" or strong ammonia or sour odor; if it does don't buy it! If the seafood department has a fishy odor, it means that sanitation procedures need to be improved.

For fresh fish, flesh should be firm. Steaks or filets should be moist with no drying or browning around the edges. Never refreeze previously frozen products. Wash fish and pat dry with a paper towel. Store, covered, on crushed ice in the coldest part of your refrigerator, use within a day. For frozen fish, be sure package is not damaged and has not been thawed. Look to see if ice crystals have formed. All seafood should be transported in a cooler or on ice from the store and immediately refrigerated or frozen. Do not thaw or marinate on your kitchen counter—do it in the refrigerator.

Live mussels, quahogs, soft shell clams—the shells should be tightly closed. Tap to see if shell closes more tightly. The neck of soft-shell clams (steamers) should show movement when touched. Live mussels, oysters and soft-shell clams may open their shells in the refrigerator. Give them a tap. Throw out those that do not close. Scrub scallops, mussels, clams or oysters in the shell with cold water just before opening or steaming them in the shell. Cook live shellfish within 24 hours.

Orchards, Bogs and Vineyards

The Rhode Island Greening

Who ever thought that a state as small as Rhode Island would develop two of the foremost agricultural products known today? One is the Rhode Island Greening which pomologists generally agree originated in Newport in the area known as Greens End, about 1748. According to Woodward and Beach, a tavern was kept by Mr. Greene who raised apple trees from seed. One of his most prized was a tree which had large green apples. As the tale goes, he always had a bowl of green apples on the bar for his guests. From Rhode Island, the Greening went to Plymouth Colony in 1765, and on to Ohio in 1796. Production of the Greening has reached number 11 in a list of 16 commercially important apples. Over 151 million pounds are grown annually.

The Greening, a medium to very large uniform apple with tough skin, is dark grassy green in color and greenish yellow when ripe. Its flesh is yellow. A tart, tender and juicy apple, it lends itself well to salads, pies, canning and freezing, making it very popular not only for home use but commercial as well.

Apple Fritters

3 large Rhode Island Greenings or other cooking apples
1 1/2 cups pancake batter
1/4 cup lemon juice
3/4 cup honey

❖ Peel and slice the apples into rings, remove the core. Dip the apple ring in the batter and cook for several minutes in hot oil until light brown. Turn and brown other side. Drain on paper towel, sprinkle with lemon juice. Place in a baking dish, top with honey and bake at 350° F for 10 to 15 minutes or until honey is hot and bubbly. Makes 4 servings.

❖ Note: Other fruits may be substituted for apples such as stewed pitted prunes, canned peach halves and pear halves.

Helen's Frozen Apple Cream

1 cup applesauce
1 teaspoon lemon juice
1/8 teaspoon cinnamon
1 cup heavy cream, whipped

❖ Blend together applesauce, lemon juice, and cinnamon. Fold in whipped heavy cream. Freeze in ice tray. Serve with sponge cake or pound cake.

Apple Crisp

6 Baldwin apples, peeled, sliced
1 cup each sugar and flour
1 teaspoon baking powder
1/2 teaspoon salt
1 egg
1/2 cup butter or margarine
Cinnamon and nutmeg

❖ Arrange apples in an ungreased 9-inch pan. Preheat oven to 350° F. In a medium bowl, mix together sugar, flour, baking power and salt with a fork. Add egg and continue mixing using fork. Put this mixture on top of apples. Melt butter, pour over apple mixture. Sprinkle with cinnamon and nutmeg. Bake 25 to 30 minutes. Serve warm or cold.

Baked Apples

This is a great way to use up oven space, when baking a meat loaf and baked potatoes or acorn squash with sausage and brown sugar. You have all the elements of an entire meal cooking all at once. Who says microwaves are everything!

6 baking apples
1/2 cup honey or sugar
1/2 cup raisins, optional
1/2 teaspoon cinnamon
1/2 teaspoon nutmeg
1 cup water

❖ Core apples without cutting through the bottom end. Peel about one third of the way down. Place in baking dish. Mix remaining ingredients, except water. Fill centers of apples. Pour water into baking dish and cover. Bake at 350° F for about 45 minutes.

Apple Macaroon Pudding

Serve hot or cold—plain or with light cream or boiled custard

3 cups applesauce
1/2 cup finely chopped almonds
1 cup crushed macaroons
2 tablespoons butter, melted

❖ Put a layer of applesauce in a buttered 1½-quart baking dish. Sprinkle with half of the almonds, then half of the macaroons into which the melted butter has been stirred. Repeat layers and bake at 350° F for 20 minutes. Serves 6.

Applesauce

❖ Wash, pare, core and cut apples into slices.

❖ In a saucepan add just enough water to keep from burning, about 1/2 cup for 6 to 8 apples.

❖ Cover and cook very slowly until tender. Mash with a hand masher or fork to make sauce smooth. Add sugar to taste.

❖ I like to add a few shakes of nutmeg and/or cinnamon and just enough sugar to taste (depends on tartness of apples).

Applesauce Plus

6 cups apple pieces, pared and cored
1 cup water
1/4 to 1/3 cup sugar
1/2 teaspoon cinnamon

❖ Cook apples in water in a covered saucepan for 10 to 15 minutes or until tender.

❖ Mash undrained apples and sugar and cinnamon to taste. Applesauce will vary in texture, juiciness and tartness with the variety used.

❖ For variety, sweeten the applesauce with honey instead of granulated sugar.

Raisin Applesauce: Add 1/4 cup raisins to the hot applesauce.

Lemon Applesauce: Add a little lemon juice to applesauce if needed for tartness. Garnish with lemon slice and sprig of mint.

Apple-Orange-Quince Marmalade

3 apples
3 oranges
3 quinces
6 cups sugar
2 cups water

❖ Cut up fruit and remove seeds. Put through grinder. Put all ingredients in a heavy saucepan.

❖ Boil for about 1/2 hour, stirring until thickened. Put in sterilized jars. Seal. Makes about 6 jars.

Fried Apple Rings

1 apple per serving
Butter or drippings

❖ Wash and core apple. Leave on skin and slice into 1/2-inch rounds.

❖ Fry in a little butter, bacon or fat from sausage. Serve as an accompaniment or garnish.

Apple Jack

Nestled in among some of the older famous farms in Northwestern Rhode Island is a newly developing orchard called Apple Jack. Owned and operated by a vivacious young couple, Anne-Marie and Jack Kachanis, this small establishment has a bit of history behind it and promises to make some in the future. Many years ago, an apple orchard owned by Harold Steere marked the boundary of Scituate, Smithfield and Glocester at the corner of Route 116. As time passed, so too did its owner.

After 14 years of overgrowth and no maintenance, a four acre orchard block was resurrected. Apple Jack began to learn the art of pruning and soon restored the trees back to a producing orchard. Since that time the land has been worked and prepared for the planting of new varieties of apples. In the coming years, watch for a partially organic orchard that will offer "pick your own" and fresh pure apple cider. Apple Jack is a must-see to bring you back to the way we were.

Swedish Apple Pie

Ann-Marie "loves to cook for a man who loves to eat." She shares her version of her mother's and her grandmother's recipe for pie.

12 to 14 apples, peeled and sliced
1 tablespoon sugar
1 teaspoon cinnamon
1 cup sugar
1 cup flour
1 egg
1/2 cup nuts
3/4 cup melted butter or margarine
1/2 cup coconut
1 teaspoon vanilla, optional

❖ Peel and pare enough apples to fill 10-inch pie dish well. Sprinkle with 1 tablespoon sugar and cinnamon. Set aside.

❖ In a small bowl combine 1 cup sugar, flour, egg, nuts, melted butter, coconut and vanilla. Pour over apples. Bake at 350° F for 45 to 50 minutes. If you really want to be different—add 1/4 cup chocolate bits!

Sour Cream Apple and Cranberry Pie

I really didn't mean to feature chefs or others that you may of heard of, but I couldn't resist this Nantucket winner, William R. Brackett, Jr., a winner of the Nantucket Cranberry Cookoff in the professional chef division. Formerly of the Jared Coffin, he is now developing new recipes at American Seasons on the island. He and his wife Brenda also own and operate The Nantucket Gourmet— a wonderful place for shopping for the home and kitchen.

1 9-inch pie shell
1 cup dried cranberries
12 to 14 McIntosh or Granny Smith apples
1 cup sour cream
1 egg
2/3 cup sugar
1/3 cup flour
Pinch of salt
1/2 teaspoon each cinnamon, allspice and nutmeg
1 cup each white and brown sugar
1/2 cup flour
1/2 cup butter, diced into 1/4-inch pieces
2/3 cup chopped walnuts

❖ Bake pie shell for 12 to 15 minutes. Plump cranberries in warm water for about 30 minutes. Peel, core and slice apples very thin. Drain cranberries. Toss apples and cranberries with mixture of next 8 ingredients. Mound in pie shell. Arrange a foil collar around the pie, place on a sheet pan and bake at 350° F for 35 minutes. Mix together remaining sugars and flour and sprinkle over filling. Arrange butter and walnuts evenly over top. Bake an additional 20 to 25 minutes. Remove and let cool at room temperature. Remove collar. Serve warm with vanilla ice cream or whipped cream. Serves 8.

Oatmeal Betty

2/3 cup flour
1/4 teaspoon salt
1/4 teaspoon baking powder
2/3 cup quick-cooking oats
2 cups canned sliced apples or peaches
2 tablespoons lemon juice
1/2 teaspoon cinnamon
1 tablespoon butter or margarine
1/3 cup brown sugar
1/4 cup vegetable oil
1/2 teaspoon vanilla

❖ Sift flour, salt and baking powder together. Mix oats into flour. Put drained peaches in a buttered 2-quart casserole, sprinkle with lemon juice and cinnamon. Dot with butter. Add brown sugar to oil, then add flour mixture and vanilla, mix until lit looks crumbly. Spread mixture over peaches. Bake at 375° F for 45 minutes. Serve hot or cold with milk or cream. Serves 4.

Know Your Apples

Best Baking Apples: Northern Spy, Rome Beauty, Winesap and Stayman.

For General Cooking: Courtland, Golden Delicious, Jonathan, MacIntosh, Northern Spy, Rome Beauty, Stayman and, last but not least, the Rhode Island Greening.

For Eating Raw: Cortland (resists browning), Red and Golden Delicious, MacIntosh, Northern Spy and Winesap.

from the U.S. Department of Agriculture

Bogs

Of all fruits, only three—the blueberry, the Concord grape and the cranberry can trace their roots in North American soil. Wild cranberries were used in many ways by the Indians. The one remaining bog which is on Martha's Vineyard owned by the Wampanoag tribe may see a new lease on life in coming years. Popular during harvest season is the cranberry festival held there. Cultivation of the cranberry began around 1810, shortly after Captain Henry Hall of Dennis, Massachusetts, noticed that the wild cranberries in his bogs grew better when beach sand blew over them. Cranberries are a unique fruit. They can only grow and survive under a very special combination of factors: they require an acid peat soil, an adequate fresh water supply, sand and a growing season that stretches from April to November. Contrary to popular belief, cranberries do not grow in water. Instead, they grow on vines in impermeable beds layered with sand, peat, gravel and clay. The beds, commonly known as "bogs," were originally made

by glacial deposits. Normally growers do not have to replant since an undamaged cranberry vine will survive indefinitely. Some in this ares are more than 150 years old. Harvest begins sometime after labor day by dry or wet harvesting. Those that are dry harvested are used for the fresh fruit market, since they have a longer shelf life. Wet harvesting is used for processed cranberries. A multimillion dollar industry is dominated by Ocean Spray Growers owned as a cooperative. Nearly 750 cranberry growers work their bogs as their business.

The Islands have their share of the market. In the little village of Greene, Rhode Island, the Greene Cranberry Company harvests its berries from a 90-acre bog which is more than a century old and is the only commercial bog in Rhode Island. Virginia Siener, one of the owners of the family enterprise, has owned the bog for the last 20 years, but has a long history of being able to use the land as descendants of Edward E. Arnold, who

was born there in 1853. Both dry and wet harvesting are used. With dedicated workers and love of the land, the family has developed a good producing bog. Hopes are for over 15,000 barrels this year; barrels are figured in the 100 pound weight.

The world's largest cranberry bog is located on Nantucket Island, covering 270 acres with 33 miles of land and ditches which provide for drainage and flooding to protect the crop. The bog is part of a tract of land covering more than a thousand acres on the Island. It has been quietly in existence since about 1857, about the time the whaling industry was fading. Many seafaring families turned to cranberry farming, as did Captain John J. Gardner and Henry Coffin, descendants of the original settlers on the Island. There have been many owners. About late 40s and early 1950s, the bog seemed to have been virtually worked out. In 1959, six of the Island's leading citizens organized Nantucket Cranberries, Inc. They have since brought back the bogs to a producing status. In 1968, The Nantucket Conservation Foundation's stewardship of its cranberry bogs began when Roy Larsen, Walter Bernecke, Jr. and Arthur Dean joined forces to purchase the assets of what was then known as Nantucket Cranberries to incorporate the Milestone Road Cranberry Bog's total of nearly 100 acres into the program of the foundation. The Windswept Cranberry Bog, a man-made bog built at the turn of the century was purchased by the Foundation in 1980. This property totals 205 acres of marsh, woodland and bogs. Forty acres are cultivated. This entire area is of natural and historical significance on Nantucket Island. The public is encouraged to visit, explore and enjoy these properties and will have a chance to see cranberrying at its best.

Cranberries All Year

Hint: During fresh cranberry season, be sure to tuck some extra packages into your freezer. Frozen cranberries may be used as successfully as fresh berries. Don't thaw the berries. Give them a quick rinse in cold water. Then grind or chop them in their frozen state or cook as you would fresh berries. Cranberry relishes, breads and desserts freeze well, so make an extra batch for your freezer.

Cranberry-Apple Jelly

7 cups cranberry apple juice
9 cups sugar
1 box powdered pectin
1/2 teaspoon margarine

❖ Sterilize jars. Put juice in a 6 to 8-quart pan. Measure sugar and set aside. Add fruit pectin and margarine to juice. Bring mixture to a full rolling boil over high heat, stirring constantly. (A full rolling boil cannot be stirred down.) Quickly add sugar to juice mixture. Bring to full rolling boil and boil for 1 minute, stirring constantly. Remove from heat. Skim off any foam. Fill all jars quickly to 1/8 inch from the top. Wipe lip of jar and cover quickly with flat lids. Screw bands on tightly. Invert jars for 5 minutes and then turn upright. Check for seal the next day, flat lid should not bulge. (If you have some that did not seal properly, store in refrigerator and use.) Makes 8 to 10 jars.

Harvest Cranberry-Apple Mold

1 3-ounce package fruit flavor gelatin
1/3 cup sugar
1/8 teaspoon cinnamon
Dash of cloves
3/4 cup boiling water
1 cup crushed ice
1 medium apple, peeled and cut in wedges
1 cup fresh cranberries

❖ Combine gelatin, sugar, seasonings and boiling water in a blender. Cover and blend at low speed until gelatin is dissolved, about 30 seconds. Add crushed ice and blend at high speed until ice is melted, about 30 seconds. Measure out 3 cups of gelatin mixture and chill until thickened. Add apples and cranberries to the remaining gelatin in blender and blend on low until fruit is broken into pieces; stir into thickened gelatin. Pour mixture into a 1-quart mold and chill until firm, at least 1 hour. Unmold on a bed of lettuce and garnish with fruit dressing or mayonnaise. Serves 6.

Crimson Cranberry Flambé

1½ cups sugar
1 cup water
2 cups fresh cranberries
¼ to ½ cup brandy or 6 to 8 sugar cubes soaked in lemon extract

❖ Bring sugar and water to boil in saucepan. When sugar dissolves, add cranberries. Simmer gently until skins pop open, about 5 minutes. When ready to serve, heat sauce in chafing dish. Pour brandy over top or place sugar cubes soaked in lemon extract on top and light. Ladle sauce over scoops of coconut ice cream or coconut ice cream balls.

Easy Coconut Ice Cream

❖ Fold 1 cup flaked or fresh grated coconut into 1 quart softened vanilla ice cream. Place in freezer until firm.

Coconut Ice Cream Balls

❖ Roll large scoops of vanilla ice cream in toasted coconut. Place in freezer until needed.

Cranberry-Orange Lattice Pie

1 pound fresh cranberries (4 cups)
2½ cups sugar
⅓ cup quick-cooking tapioca
1 teaspoon cinnamon
⅛ teaspoon ground cloves
½ teaspoon salt
1 cup orange juice
½ cup diced orange sections
1 tablespoon margarine
½ teaspoon vanilla
Pastry for 2-crust pie

❖ In a saucepan, combine cranberries with sugar, tapioca, spices, salt and orange juice. Cover and cook over medium heat until skins pop, about 6 to 8 minutes. Remove from heat. Stir in orange sections and vanilla. Prepare pastry, rolling half of pastry out to line a 9-inch pie plate. Turn cranberry mixture into pie shell and dot with margarine. Roll remaining pastry ⅛ inch thick. Cut into ½ inch wide strips and arrange over pie in lattice fashion. Trim and flute edges. Bake at 450° F for 10 minutes, then reduce temperature to 350° F and bake for 20 to 25 minutes longer or until crust is golden.

Cranberry Relish

Actually this should be called Cranberry Orange Relish—but this is the way Gram gave me the receipt.

1 cup raw cranberries, chopped
1 small orange, chopped skin and all
½ cup sugar
½ teaspoon lemon juice

❖ Mix chopped ingredients with sugar and lemon juice. (Be sure and include the juice from the orange.) Put in a clean tightly covered jar and serve tomorrow when flavors have gone together. Will last in the refrigerator for 3 to 4 weeks. Recipe may be doubled or tripled. One 12-ounce package of cranberries makes 4 cups of relish.

Jellied Cranberry-Orange Relish

3 cups fresh cranberries (12-ounce package)
¾ cup orange juice with pulp
1 cup sugar
1 large orange, ground

❖ In a heavy saucepan, boil for 5 minutes or until cranberries are popped, stirring constantly. Sauce should start to thicken. Put in sterilized jars. Refrigerate.

Giant Cranberry Turnover

Filling:
1 12-ounce bag fresh or frozen cranberries
2 firm pears, peeled, cored and cubed
1/2 cup dried apricots, chopped
1 cup dark raisins, optional
1/2 cup sugar for tart, 3/4 cup for sweet
1 teaspoon cinnamon
1/2 cup orange juice
1/4 cup chopped walnuts
1 1/2 tablespoons orange liqueur

Pastry:
1 17 1/2-ounce package frozen puff pastry
1 egg
1 tablespoon water
2 teaspoons sugar

❖ In a saucepan, combine cranberries, pears, apricots, raisins, sugar, cinnamon and orange juice. Bring to a boil and cook for 8 minutes; stir until thick. Remove and stir in walnuts and liqueur. Cool to room temperature. This mixture may be frozen for 1 month. Roll 1 sheet pastry to a 12-inch square and place on a 14x17-inch baking sheet. Put filling in center of square. Beat egg and water and brush on exposed pastry. Roll second piece of pastry the same way, put on top of filling. Trim to 10 inches. Brush with remaining egg. Using the tines of a fork, press edges together to seal. Make slits on top. Use leftover pastry to make bows and slits like holly. Sprinkle with sugar. Chill for 30 minutes. Bake at 400° F for 15 minutes, reduce heat to 350° F and bake for 20 to 25 minutes longer or until golden. If it starts to brown too soon, cover with foil. Serve warm with vanilla ice cream or whipped cream.

Dietetic Cranberry Sauce

4 cups fresh cranberries
1 1/2 cups water
4 teaspoons liquid sweetener

❖ Combine cranberries, water and sweetener in a saucepan.

❖ Bring to a boil, lower heat and simmer until berries pop open (about 10 minutes).

❖ Chill to serve. Makes 1 to 1 1/2 pints.

Cranberry Sherbet

4 cups cranberries
3 cups water

❖ Cook until soft. Put through sieve. Stir in 1 1/2 cups sugar.

❖ Heat until sugar dissolves. Cool.

❖ Add 1/2 cup orange juice and 1/4 cup lemon juice. Freeze.

❖ I stir it several times when it thickens and it is much smoother.

Chicama Vineyards

Chicama Vineyards, owned and operated by George and Catherine Mathiesen, is the oldest continuously operating winery and vineyard in New England. Founded in 1971, in West Tisbury, Martha's Vineyard, as a family business on 18 acres, their output is approximately 15,000 gallons a year featuring Cape Cod White, Cranberry Apple and Sea Mist—a sparkling wine much like a champagne. Open on Saturdays from January to April and Monday through Saturday from May to December featuring tours, tastings and a gift and Christmas shop. Well, worth a stop when you're on Martha's Vineyard.

Chicama Vineyard Jamaica Zinger Pasta

Tasty and quick, but one catch—you must order Zinger oil from Chicama Vineyards, Martha's Vineyard.

1/2 **pound linguine or spaghetti**
2 to 3 **tablespoons Jamaica Zinger oil**
1/4 **cup chopped parsley**
1/2 **cup Parmesan cheese**
1/4 **cup chopped basil**

❖ Cook pasta using package directions. Put drained pasta in a warm bowl; drizzle with Jamaica Zinger oil and toss to mix thoroughly. Sprinkle with parsley, Parmesan cheese and basil; toss again. Serve immediately with Chicama Zinfandel. Serves 2.

Barbecue Marinade: Mix 1/4 cup Zinger oil, 1/4 cup red wine vinegar and 1 large clove garlic, chopped.

Basting Sauce: Mix 1/4 cup Zinger oil, 1/4 cup fresh orange juice, 1 tablespoon honey and grated rind of 1 orange.

Jamaica Scampi: Quickly sauté 1/2 pound peeled, deveined shrimp in 2 tablespoons each Zinger oil and butter. Serve over pasta or rice.

Diamond Hill Vineyards

Pete and Claire Berntson of Cumberland founded their "budding" winery in 1976 with a number of varietal wines featuring an excellent fruit wine from the Rhode Island Greening. A growing operation, Diamond Hill has 41/2 acres of Pinot, and is establishing a six acre organic wine orchard which includes apples, peaches, pears and plums. One of my current favorites is their peach wine. The Berntsons say, "Watch for our Pinot Noir which we treat as a favorite child by providing special care to help it withstand New England winters in years to come." They also have festivals throughout the year, tours and tastings, and cater special events at their vineyard. Another unique feature available from their salesroom is personalized labels for special occasions.

Diamond Hill Chicken with Blueberry Wine

4 boneless chicken breasts
Flour
Salt and pepper
6 to 8 tablespoons clarified butter
2 tablespoons chopped onion
1 to 1¼ cups Diamond Hill Blueberry Wine
Cinnamon
Butter
Parsley for garnish

❖ Sprinkle chicken with flour, salt and pepper. Shake off excess flour. Put clarified butter in the bottom of a large frying pan. Heat butter until it starts to darken. Place prepared chicken in butter. Sauté about 3 to 4 minutes, then turn. Cook about 3 to 4 more minutes depending how thick chicken is. Chicken should be "spongy" to the touch when cooked. Do not overcook. Remove chicken and keep warm. Quickly sauté onion in remaining butter in pan for a few minutes, then add blueberry wine. Boil rapidly until liquid becomes a light syrup. Add cinnamon to bring out the spiciness of the blueberry. Remove from heat and blend in 2 tablespoons butter. Pour over cooked chicken breasts. Garnish with parsley. Serves 4.

❖ Note: To clarify butter, put 1 stick of butter in a saucepan over medium-high heat until butter foams. Remove from heat and skim off foam.

Nantucket Vineyards

Nantucket Vineyards feature a wonderful white wine named Nantucket Sleigh Ride which is only available on the island and was developed by Dean and Melissa Long, owners. They are a young couple who decided farm life and Nantucket were for them. They decided to start a vineyard on the island. They, as other vineyard owners, have expanded their vineyards as well as their expertise in producing quality wines from this area. The tasting room is open daily.

Nantucket Vineyard Wild Rice à la Ros

Oil and butter
¾ to 1 pound mushrooms, sliced
1½ cups chopped celery
1½ cups chopped onions
¾ cups minced green pepper
3 cups (1 pound) uncooked wild rice
3 cups bouillon or white wine
1 teaspoon salt
Pepper to taste
¾ teaspoon Worcestershire sauce
¾ teaspoon catsup
2 tablespoons minced parsley
5 juniper berries, optional

❖ Place rice in sieve and rinse under running water; drain. Heat oil in large skillet. Sauté mushrooms. Add onions, celery and green pepper. Sauté until soft. Add remaining ingredients. Simmer, covered, for 45 minutes to 1 hour. Add additional liquid if needed. Spoon into casserole. Bake, covered, at 325° F for 20 to 25 minutes or until fluffy.

❖ Note: May be reheated in microwave. May be served cold. May substitute 1½ cups white long-grain rice for half the wild rice.

Prudence Island Vineyards

Prudence Island Vineyards is located at Sunset Hill Farm. Since 1973, the William Bacon family have operated this small vineyard on Prudence Island in Portsmouth. On only 12 acres, they have a quality Chardonnay. Currently the Bacons are running a retail shop, but by appointment only.

Sakonnet Vineyards

This recipe is courtesy of Susan Samson, proprietress of Sakonnet Vineyards. "The Vineyard was established in 1975. It has become a New England pioneer in the production of fine wines. Sakonnet has evolved a distinct New England style of wine, due to the favorable interaction of soil and climate along the Southeastern New England coast. Rhode Island Red

wine is composed of Chancellor and Pinot Noir grapes fermented in stainless steel and aged in small oak barrels. The smooth long finish provides an excellent accompaniment to roast lamb, beef and pasta." Open year round, Sakonnet ships anywhere from 62 West Main Road, Little Compton, Rhode Island 02837. Tele. (401) 635-8486.

Sakonnet Vineyards' Rhode Island Red Bourguignon

1/2 pound country-style bacon
1 tablespoon olive oil
3 1/2 pounds top or bottom round
2 carrots and 2 onions, sliced
1/2 teaspoon salt
1/4 teaspoon pepper
2 tablespoons flour
3 1/2 cup Sakonnet Vineyards' Rhode Island Red Wine
2 to 3 cups beef bouillon
1 1/2 tablespoons tomato paste
2 cloves garlic, mashed
1/2 teaspoon thyme
1 bay leaf, crumbled
1   10 1/2-ounce package frozen baby onions
1 pound fresh mushrooms, quartered
Butter for sautéing

❖   Preheat oven to 325° F. Cut bacon into 1 1/2-inch strips; sauté in olive oil over moderate heat in a 9 or 10-inch Dutch oven for 2 to 3 minutes or until light brown. Remove bacon and reserve. Cut beef into 2-inch cubes and sauté in rendered oil and bacon fat until brown on all sides. Remove and set aside. Sauté carrots and onions; sprinkle with salt, pepper and flour. Toss lightly to coat. Brown lightly on top of stove. Do not burn. Stir in wine with drippings and enough bouillon to barely cover meat. Add next 4 ingredients. Bring to a simmer on top of stove, then cover and put in lower part of oven. Simmer very slowly for 3 to 4 hours. The meat is done when pierced easily with a fork.

❖   While the beef is cooking, prepare the frozen onions according to the package directions; sauté the mushrooms in butter. When meat is done, pour contents of casserole through a sieve over a saucepan. Rinse casserole and return beef and bacon to it. Put prepared onions and mushrooms over meat. Defat sauce. Sauce should be thick enough to coat a spoon lightly.

To thicken, boil down rapidly. To thin, add a few tablespoons of the red wine. Pour sauce over meat and vegetables. Recipe can be made in advance to this point. For later serving, cover and refrigerate when cooled. Before serving, simmer very slowly for about 10 minutes, basting meat and vegetables a few times. For immediate serving, simmer very slowly for about 10 minutes, basting the meat and vegetables a few times. Serve immediately with egg noodles and fresh peas.

Vinland Wine Cellars

Vinland Wine Cellars, owned and operated by Captain Richard Alexander and his wife Hope, feature holiday baskets, glasses, custom labels and holiday wines. Tours and tastings are available daily in their Portsmouth retail shop. A good year for the vineyard, over 40 tons of fruit was harvested. Established in 1988 as a vineyard

including Hopelands, their tasting room opened in 1989 in the Eastgate Center, East Main Road, Middletown, opposite the Newport Airport.

Vinland Chicken in Wine

An original recipe from Hope Alexander of Vinland Wine Cellars, Middletown, Rhode Island. A favorite for a quick meal or entertaining.

4 chicken breasts, boned and skinned
2 to 3 tablespoons safflower oil or
    margarine
Garlic salt
Pepper
1/2 cup Vinlands Seyval wine
    (dry white wine)

❖ Wash and dry chicken breasts. Heat oil in a large frying pan and cook chicken until lightly browned on both sides, about 10 to 15 minutes depending on size. Do not over-cook. Sprinkle lightly with garlic salt and pepper. Add wine. Baste and turn chicken, cover pan. Cook for 5 more minutes. Serve on warm plates with rice. Spoon wine sauce over each piece of chicken. Serves 4.

Newport Hospitality White Wine Jelly

Another favorite recipe using wine from Vinland is a Wine Jelly using Newport Hospitality White Wine. This jelly is just great with chicken, lamb, veal or fish. The recipe was developed for Vinland by Margaret Carr.

4 cups sugar
1 1/2 teaspoons grated orange rind
1/2 cup fresh orange juice
2 tablespoons fresh lemon juice
1 1/2 cups Vinland Newport
    Hospitality White wine
1/2 3-ounce bottle liquid fruit pectin

❖ Combine all ingredients except the pectin in a large pan. Stir over moderate heat, constantly until the sugar melts and the mixture comes to a full rolling boil (one that when stirred can't be knocked down). Boil hard for 2 minutes, skimming off the foam. Seal in hot sterilized glasses. Makes about 7 half-pint glasses.

Dandelion Wine Ascanio

(*Private Middletown vintner*)

4 quarts dandelion flowers
1 cup sugar
2 sliced oranges
2 sliced lemons
1 pound raisins
3/4 yeast cake
1 small bottle maraschino cherries

❖ Get a 5-gallon bottle and fit it with stopper and tubing. Collect dandelion flowers, wash with cold water. Place the flowers in a large container such as a lobster pan and add 4 quarts boiling water. Cover and let stand overnight. Strain and squeeze flowers. Place the dandelion liquid in the 5 gallon bottle. Dissolve 1 cup sugar in 1 quart of the liquid. Add oranges, lemons and raisins to dandelion liquid. Add yeast cake which has been dissolved in 1/2 cup warm water. Add 1 bottle maraschino cherries with juice.

❖ Stopper the 5-gallon bottle and place the end of the hose in a 2 liter soda bottle that is half filled with

water. Let stand for 12 days. Observe daily for bubbling, when bubbling stops, test for sweetness. If not sweet enough add a quarter cup of sugar dissolved in a half cup of water. Stopper and let stand for 2 months. Strain the mixture. (Fruits are delicious.) Bottle the liquid keeping the cap finger tight. Tighten the cap when the bubbling stops. Makes 1 gallon of wine. *Prosit salute!*

Fruit Wine

2 16-ounce cans frozen 100% grape juice concentrate
1 cup sugar
3/4 yeast cake

❖ Get a 5-gallon bottle and fit it with a stopper and tubing.

❖ Make grape juice according to directions on can. Dissolve 1 cup of sugar in a quart of grape juice and set aside. Add the liquid to the 5-gallon bottle, if a hydrometer is available adjust the specific gravity to 1.10 or 24 Brix with prepared sugar solution. If no hydrometer is available add the entire sugar solution and 3/4 cup yeast dissolved

in 1/2 cup warm water (not hot). Stopper the 5-gallon bottle and place the end of the hose in a 2 liter soda bottle that is half filled with water. Let stand for 12 days. Observe daily for bubbling, when bubbly stops let the solution stand for 2 months. Bottle the liquid. Keep the cap finger tight. Tighten the cap when the bubbling stops.

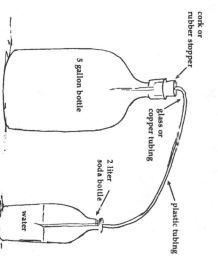

cork or rubber stopper
5 gallon bottle
glass or copper tubing
2 liter soda bottle
plastic tubing
water

Island Heritage: Cooks from Many Lands

Armenian Eggplant (Dolma)

4 onions, chopped
1/2 cup olive oil
1/2 cup rice
1 bunch parsley
3 pounds eggplant, peeled and chopped into 1/2-inch pieces
2 cups stewed tomatoes
Salt and pepper

❖ In a heavy pan, fry onions in olive oil until light brown. Add rice and cook for 10 minutes. Add chopped parsley. Remove from pan. Put back in pan alternating rice with eggplant in layers. Pour over tomatoes, 1 cup water seasoned with salt and pepper. Cook slowly for about 1/2 hour or until eggplant is soft but not mushy.

Canadian Brown Yeast Bread

From a New Brunswick Home Economist we met on our honeymoon in 1970. This bread is not to be confused with New England Brown Bread which is served with beans.

2 1/2 cups boiling water
1 1/2 cups oatmeal
1/2 cup shortening
4 teaspoons salt
1 cup scalded milk
2/3 cup molasses
1/2 cup sugar
2 packages yeast
1/4 cup lukewarm water
1 cup whole wheat flour
9 to 10 cups all-purpose flour

❖ Pour boiling water over oatmeal. Add shortening, salt, scalded milk, molasses and sugar. Stir well and cool to lukewarm. Soften yeast in 1/4 cup warm water. When oatmeal mixture is cool, stir in whole wheat flour, yeast and 3 cups all-purpose flour. Beat well and continue adding remainder of flour, reserving about 2 cups to use when kneading. When well mixed, turn out on a floured board and continue to knead 10 to 15 minutes using as much flour as needed to make a firm ball. Put in an clean oiled bowl and turn on all sides. Let rise until doubled in bulk, about 2 to 2 1/2 hours. Punch down. Divide dough into halves, knead a little more, then shape into 2 loaves. Put into greased loaf pans and cover with a towel. Place in a warm place and let rise until doubled in bulk. Bake at 350° F for 45 minutes to 1 hour. Bread is done when outside is tapped and sounds hollow.

"Just Above Water"

The *Tow* family of Providence was probably one of the best known for their Chinese food at the Ming Garden—traditional but so delicious. Yat always greeted his patrons at the door. One afternoon my husband, with a business associate was met by Yat. He asked "How's business, Yat?" He replied, "You know, Mr. Dean, just keep head above water."

Well, the following is a recipe from the Year of the Ram, which Yat shared with us, and if you try this recipe you *will know that his business was right on top—not just above water. The family now owns and operates The Great House in Warwick.*

Stir-Fried Beef and Broccoli

2 tablespoons soy sauce
1 tablespoon dry sherry
1/4 teaspoon white pepper
3/4 pound flank steak
1/2 cup plus 1 tablespoon peanut oil
4 cups broccoli florets
1/2 cup sliced onion
2 tablespoons cornstarch
1/4 cup water

❖ In a medium bowl, stir together soy sauce, sherry and pepper.

❖ Slice flank steak across the grain in thin slices. Add to soy mixture, stir to coat well.

❖ In wok or a large skillet, heat 5 tablespoons of oil over medium-high heat. Sprinkle steak strips into wok; cook and stir until meat browns. Remove to platter; keep warm.

❖ Pour 4 tablespoons oil in wok, add broccoli and onion. Cook, stirring constantly, about 3 minutes or until tender-crisp. Remove from pan and keep warm. Add remaining oil to pan; heat.

❖ Stir together cornstarch and water until smooth. Add to pan. Stir constantly. Bring to a boil for 1 minute.

❖ Return broccoli and steak strips to pan and toss until mixture is heated throughout. Serve with rice. Makes 4 servings.

Lemon Chicken

1 to 1 1/2 pounds boneless chicken
1/2 teaspoon salt
1/4 teaspoon MSG, optional
1 egg
1/2 cup cornstarch
Oil for deep frying
Lemon Sauce

❖ Flatten the boneless chicken with a meat tenderizer or the flat side of a knife.

❖ Cut chicken into 4x1 1/2-inch strips 1/2 inch thick. Place chicken strips in

mixture of salt and MSG; let stand for about 10 minutes. Remove from dish and dip chicken in egg mixture and then coat with cornstarch.

❖ Pan fry in 1/2 inch of fat, if you do not want to deep-fry. Place cooked chicken on a platter and add Lemon Sauce to top of chicken. Garnish with parsley. Serve immediately.

Lemon Sauce

1/4 cup margarine
1 cup water
3 tablespoons sugar
1 tablespoon cornstarch
4 tablespoons lemon juice
2 lemons, sliced

❖ Combine first 5 ingredients for lemon sauce in heavy saucepan and heat over medium heat until margarine is melted and mixture is thickened.

❖ Sauce will be of medium consistency. Add lemon slices.

Chicken Spring Rolls

1 large boneless chicken breast
2 tablespoons oil
6 ounces chopped fresh mushrooms
1/2 cup bamboo shoots, minced
1/2 cup minced onion
8 sheets phyllo dough
Oil for brushing phyllo

❖ Cut chicken into strips. Heat oil in large frying pan and cook chicken until meat turns white. Then add mushrooms, bamboo shoots and minced onion. Cook for 1 to 2 minutes. Mix thoroughly and remove from heat. Allow mixture to cool before wrapping. Cut each phyllo sheet into thirds. Brush 1 sheet of phyllo with oil, fold in half to form a square. Brush again with oil. Place about 1 tablespoon of cooled filling in lower corner. Fold bottom of strip diagonally to form a triangle. Continue folding phyllo strip alternately from side to side to form a triangle pocket until all dough is used. Place on an un-greased cookie sheet. Brush tops lightly with oil. Bake at 400° F for 12 to 15 minutes or until golden brown. Be careful not to overcook.

❖ Note: May be deep fried but much easier in oven. Phyllo dough dries out very fast. Follow directions on box for handling. Cover with waxed paper when working with dough.

Hot and Sour Soup

Soup can be made ahead of time and reheated gently on range or in the microwave.

6 cups chicken broth
1/4 pound ground pork
1/4 cup thinly sliced bamboo shoots
1/2 cup sliced mushrooms
1 cup tofu, thinly sliced
1 teaspoon soy sauce
3 tablespoons vinegar
1 egg, beaten
2 tablespoons cornstarch dissolved in 3 tablespoons water
1/4 cup scallions, chopped
3 tablespoons chopped green chilies
1 teaspoon oil

❖ Combine chicken broth, ground pork, bamboo shoots and mush-rooms in a large pot. Bring to a boil and cook for 5 to 6 minutes, stirring to break up the pork. Add sliced tofu and cook gently for 1 minute. Add soy sauce and vinegar. Add cornstarch, stir gently and bring to a slow boil. Add scallions, chilies and oil just before serving. Makes 4 to 6 servings.

Aichu's Sweet and Sour Pork

1 pound boneless pork

Marinade:
1/2 teaspoon salt
1 1/2 teaspoons soy sauce
1 tablespoon cornstarch
1 tablespoon cold water
1 egg yolk

2 green peppers, sliced
4 slices pineapple
1 cup (about) oil
1/2 cup cornstarch
2 tablespoons oil
1 carrot, sliced

Seasoning Sauce:
2 tablespoons white vinegar
4 tablespoons sugar
4 tablespoons catsup
5 tablespoons cold water
1 teaspoon oil

Danish Meatballs with Onion Sauce

Good served with boiled baby new potatoes and green beans.

1/2 cup dry bread crumbs
1 cup milk
1 egg, beaten
1 medium onion, chopped
1 pound ground beef or 1/2 pound veal and pork ground together
1 teaspoon salt
1/8 teaspoon allspice or nutmeg
3 tablespoons butter

❖ Soak crumbs in milk for about 10 minutes. Add beaten egg. Mix with onion, ground meat and seasonings. Shape into small balls with tablespoon. Brown in butter; when brown, simmer, covered tightly, until cooked through. Serve in a chafing dish with Onion Sauce.

Onion Sauce

1 1/2 cups sliced white onions
1/4 cup butter
2 tablespoons flour
1/4 teaspoon salt
1 1/2 cups milk

❖ Cook onions in butter over low heat until transparent. Stir in flour and salt. Add milk gradually, stirring constantly. Cook until mixture bubbles and thickens. Serves 6.

Danish Sand Bakkels

1 cup shortening or use 1/2 cup butter and 1/2 cup shortening
1 cup granulated sugar
1 egg, unbeaten
1 teaspoon almond extract
2 1/2 cups flour

❖ Cream shortening, add sugar and cream well. Add egg and extract. Add the flour to make a stiff dough. Pinch off a small ball of dough, place it in center of sand bakkel tin. Press dough evenly. Bake at 375° F for 15 minutes or until browned. Cool before removing from tins. To remove, invert the tin and tap gently. Clean tins with dry cloth only.

❖ Fillings: Prepared puddings with whipped cream garnish; lemon meringue; mince; or, fruit with currant glaze made by melting currant or apple jelly and drizzling over top.

❖ Pound pork with the back of a cleaver (this is to tenderize the pork), then cut into 1-inch squares. Soak with marinade for at least 1/2 hour.

❖ Cut green peppers into halves, remove seed and membrane and cut into 1-inch squares. Cut pineapple slices into 1-inch squares. Set aside.

❖ Heat 1 cup oil in skillet. While oil is heating, coat each piece of pork in 1/2 cup cornstarch. When oil is ready, fry pork until brown and done (about 2 minutes), remove from skillet. Reheat oil; fry once more until crispy. Remove pork and drain oil from frying pan.

❖ Put 2 tablespoons new oil in skillet; fry carrot, green peppers and pineapple, stirring constantly. Add mixture of seasoning sauce ingredients, stirring constantly until thickened. Turn off the heat. Add pork; mix well and serve immediately or cool and freeze in film. Reheat in microwave for 1 minute or if frozen, reheat for 4 minutes on High.

English Maids of Honor

Oh, so British! Cake and jelly tarts for a nibble or at teatime.

Batter:
1/2 cup margarine
1 cup sugar
1/4 teaspoon salt
1 teaspoon vanilla
2 eggs
1 1/2 cups flour
2 teaspoons baking powder
2/3 cup milk

❖ Cream the margarine and sugar until fluffy. Add salt and vanilla, beat. Add the eggs, 1 at a time beating well after each addition. Sift the flour and baking powder together and add alternately to creamed mixture.

Pastry:
2 cups flour
1/4 teaspoon salt
3/4 cup shortening
6 to 8 tablespoons cold water

❖ Sift flour and salt together, cut in shortening with a pastry blender or 2 knives. Add water, mixing in with knife. Do not handle too much. Roll out and cut with a floured cutter or glass so it will fit a muffin tin. Line muffin tins with pastry. Put 1/2 teaspoon jelly of your choice, I like quince or cranberry, then drop in a spoonful of batter. Tin should only be 3/4 full. Bake at 350° F for 20 to 25 minutes or until the cake tests done.

Wickford Gourmet Foods

This is the House recipe which is a variation of a traditional English Scone recipe. Joe Dubé and his wife, Donna, have developed a delightful business in the heart of historic Wickford, Rhode Island, which includes Wickford Gourmet Foods, featuring a touch of Europe and Wickford Gourmet Kitchen and Table. Everything from lunch to stay-or-go, catering, baskets to deliver anywhere (particularly if you would like a real Rhode Island Basket) as well as cookware, cookbooks, coffee, linens and tableware, etc. They even have a bridal and gift registry.

Wickford Gourmet Breakfast Scones

3 cups flour
1 1/2 tablespoons baking powder
1/4 teaspoon salt
1/2 cup sugar
6 tablespoons butter
1/2 cup raisins
3 eggs plus 1 for glaze
1/2 cup milk
Sugar

❖ Sift flour, baking powder, salt and sugar together. Cut in butter. Add raisins. Add 3 eggs and milk making a soft dough. Handle as little as possible.

❖ Roll out to 1/2-inch thickness. Cut into wedges and brush with egg glaze. Dust with sugar, place on ungreased baking sheet.

❖ Bake at 375° F for 12 to 17 minutes. Makes approximately 1 to 1 1/2 dozen.

German Apple Cake

1 cup light brown sugar
2 tablespoons flour
2 tablespoons margarine
2 teaspoons cinnamon
1/2 cup sugar
1/4 cup shortening
1 egg
1/2 cup milk
11/2 cups unsifted flour
2 teaspoons baking powder
1/2 teaspoon salt
2 cups thinly sliced apples

❖ Mix first 4 ingredients for topping and set aside.

❖ Combine sugar, shortening and egg. Beat thoroughly and stir in milk. Mix flour, baking powder and salt, stirring into egg mixture just until smooth. Spread half of batter into a greased 9-inch baking pan. Cover with half the apples. Top with half of topping mixture. Add remaining batter, apples and topping. Bake at 375° F for 45 to 50 minutes.

French Prune Cookies

Dough:
1 8-ounce package cream cheese
2 sticks butter, melted
3 cups flour

Filling:
11/2 pound pitted prunes, cooked and drained
1 10-ounce jar maraschino cherries, drained and chopped
1 8-ounce can crushed pineapple, drained
1 cup chopped nuts
1 teaspoon vanilla extract
1/4 cup brandy, optional

❖ Cream together room temperature cream cheese with butter. Mix with flour until well blended. Refrigerate for 1/2 hour. Mix together all filling ingredients, set aside. Roll dough to 1/8-inch thickness. Use a 3-inch round or square cutter. Put 1/2 teaspoon of filling in center of each; fold over and press together. Bake at 350° F on ungreased cookie sheet for 15 to 20 minutes or until light brown. When cool dust with confectioners' sugar. Yields about 80.

Estonian Vegetable Salad (Rosolje)

This recipe was served at our local preservation society meeting some years ago and loved by all. As the story goes, this editor of a local cookbook was to include the recipe for all to enjoy—well, through an oversight the recipe was omitted much to my dismay and the contributor's. Hilja, I thank you for the recipe and here it is in print for everyone to enjoy who reads this book.

4 to 6 cold boiled potatoes, diced
2 to 3 hard-boiled eggs, chopped
3/4 cup boiled cold beets, diced
1 medium sour raw apple, diced
1/2 cup dill pickle, chopped
1 cup boiled or baked meat, diced

Sauce:
3/4 cup sour cream
1/2 cup mayonnaise
2 tablespoons white vinegar
1 teaspoon hot or Dijon mustard

❖ Mix all ingredients and chill before serving on a bed of crisp greens.

Koenig's Kuchen

2 sticks margarine
1 cup less 2 tablespoons sugar
5 large eggs
1 teaspoon vanilla
1 teaspoon grated lemon rind
4 cups unbleached flour
3 teaspoons baking powder
1 cup milk
1/2 cup raisins
1/2 cup currants
3/4 cup nuts (walnuts or pecans)
2 ounces citron, optional

❖ Cream together margarine and sugar until fluffy. Add eggs, 1 at a time, add vanilla and lemon rind. Mix well. Add flour, 1 cup at a time, baking powder and milk to make a dough. Add raisins, currants, nuts and citron. Mix. Pour into greased and floured loaf pans. Bake at 350° F for 45 minutes. Reduce temperature to 325° F and bake for 15 minutes. Let cool on wire rack. Makes 2 loaves.

❖ Note: Keeps very well.

Sigrid's Linzer Torte

Guten Appetit!

1 2/3 cups flour
1 3/4 cups ground almonds
3/4 cup sugar
2 tablespoons cocoa
1 teaspoon cinnamon
1/2 teaspoon ground cloves
1 teaspoon vanilla
1 egg
1 ounce Kirsch liqueur
2 sticks butter or margarine, cut into small cubes
1   16-ounce jar raspberry jam
1 teaspoon lemon or lime juice
1 egg yolk

❖ Preheat oven to 375° F.

❖ Mix dry ingredients together.

❖ Make a well in center for vanilla, egg and Kirsch. Add quickly the cubed butter. (Can be made in the food processor for quick mixing.)

❖ Let stand in refrigerator for at least an hour. At this point may go in freezer until ready to use.

❖ Roll out half the dough to fit the pan bottoms to the thickness for sugar cookies. Roll out the rest of the dough and create 1/2 inch wide strips for circle around inside edge of pan.

❖ Spread jam on the center and top with lattice trim or cutout like stars or hearts (seasonal). Brush dough with egg yolk.

❖ Bake at 375° F for 15 minutes then reduce temperature to 350° F and continue baking for 45 minutes.

❖ Recipe will make: two 10-inch springforms or three 7½-inch springforms or one 12-inch springform and one 7½-inch springform.

German Christmas Stollen

Not the cheapest, but without a doubt, one of the best I have had, and it stays fresh throughout the holidays if not eaten all at one sitting. Thanks Margot!

3 cups golden raisins
3 cups dark raisins
1 cup finely diced glazed fruit
1 cup rum
3 packages dry yeast
1/2 cup warm water
1 1/2 cups milk, scalded then cooled to lukewarm
8 cups flour
2 sticks butter, softened
1 cup sugar
4 eggs
1 teaspoon salt
Grated rind of 1 lemon
1/2 teaspoon nutmeg
1 tablespoon vanilla
2 cups butter, melted
1 cup sugar
1 teaspoon cinnamon
Confectioners' sugar

❖ Soak raisins and glazed fruit in rum for 3 days. Stir fruit once to make sure it is completely soaked. In small mixing bowl, place yeast and warm water; mix until yeast dissolves. Add warm milk and 1 cup of flour, mixing well. Cover and place in a warm area until light and bubbly.

❖ In a large mixing bowl, cream softened butter and sugar until light and fluffy. Add eggs, one at a time, beating well after each addition. Mix in salt, lemon rind and yeast mixture. Stir in nutmeg, vanilla and flour, 1 cup at a time, stirring well after each addition. Turn dough out onto a floured board and knead until smooth, about 10 to 15 minutes. Add drained, rum soaked fruit to dough and knead until evenly distributed. Place dough in a greased bowl. Turn dough over so it is greased on all sides. Cover with a piece of wax paper and towel. Allow to rise in a warm spot until doubled in bulk, about 1 to 1 1/2 hours. Punch dough down and divide into 3 equal parts. Let rise for 10 minutes. Roll each out to a strip about 12x8 inches. Brush with 2 tablespoons melted butter and fold each strip by bringing one long side over to the center and pressing the edge down. Fold the other long side across it. Overlap about 1 inch. Press edge gently to keep it in place. Taper ends of the loaf and pat sides gently to mound it in center. The finished loaf should be about 4 inches wide and 13 inches long, in semi-crescent shape.

❖ Place stollen on lightly greased cookie sheets and brush with melted butter, cover lightly and allow to rise for 1 hour or until doubled. Bake loaves on middle rack at 350° F for 35 minutes or until golden brown and crusty. (Should sound slightly hollow when tapped.) When removed from oven, puncture each stollen about 12 times with a dowel, or the handle of a wooden spoon. Brush with melted butter so it soaks in thoroughly. Sprinkle liberally with mixture of sugar and cinnamon. Remove to wire racks to cool completely. Before serving sprinkle generously with confectioners' sugar. Makes 3 very large loaves.

❖ Note: If for gift giving, you may want to divide dough into 6 smaller loaves. Wrap when cool.

Artemis' Greek Quince Almond Spoon Sweets

(Glyka Kythoni Me Amygthala)

3 cups prepared quince
3 cups water
2 geranium leaves
3 cups sugar
1/2 cup blanched almonds
1 teaspoon vanilla

❖ Peel and cut quince very thin like spaghetti using a hand grater. Discard the core.

❖ Put prepared quince in a heavy saucepan with water and geranium leaves. Bring to a boil and simmer until quince is soft and liquid turns rosey red.

❖ Add sugar, stirring constantly until mixture thickens, about 15 to 20 minutes.

❖ Add 1/2 cup almonds and vanilla. Pour into sterilized jars. Seal. Makes about 3 pints.

Greek Pork Curry Appetizer

1/2 pound ground pork or ground round
1 tablespoon oil
1/2 cup chopped onions
1/2 cup chopped bamboo shoots
1 teaspoon curry powder
1/4 teaspoon sugar
4 tablespoons catsup
10 sheets phyllo
Oil for brushing phyllo

❖ In a large skillet, heat about 1 tablespoon oil and brown pork. Drain. Add onions, bamboo shoots and seasonings. Mix ingredients together and cook for 2 to 3 minutes longer. Set aside and cool until ready to use.

❖ Cut phyllo into thirds lengthwise and stack. Cover with waxed paper and a damp cloth or paper towel. Brush a single sheet of phyllo with oil. Fold in half lengthwise. Brush top with oil. Put 1 teaspoon filling on bottom of strip. Fold bottom of strip diagonally to form a triangle. Continue folding phyllo strip alternately from side to side to form a triangle pocket until all dough is used.

❖ Place on an ungreased cookie sheet. Baste tops lightly with oil.

❖ Bake at 400° F for 12 to 15 minutes or until golden brown. Be careful not to overcook.

Tulip's Greek Rice Pudding

"Tulips is the best, probably because she makes enough to serve 25 when she makes a batch for this family's restaurant in West Warwick."

1/2 cup raw rice
Pinch of salt
1 quart milk
4 egg yolks
3/4 cup sugar
Grated rind of 1 lemon or lime, optional
1 teaspoon vanilla extract
Ground cinnamon

❖ Parboil rice in 1/2 cup water with a pinch of salt for 10 minutes; drain. Add drained rice to milk and simmer over low heat, stirring occasionally, for 45 minutes to 1 hour. Beat eggs with sugar.

❖ Remove rice mixture from heat and very slowly stir in the egg yolks. Add grated rind and return to low heat; stirring constantly until mixture is creamy and thick.

❖ Add vanilla, mix well and pour into a dessert bowl. Sprinkle with cinnamon; cool. Serve with whipped cream. Serves 6.

Broccoli di Rabe

Although broccoli di rabe was an ever present vegetable in ethnic households, it wasn't until recently that it has become a popular food. You either like rabe or you don't because of its strong flavor. For some, rabe is an acquired taste.

1 pound fresh rabe or mustard greens
1/4 cup olive oil
3 cloves garlic, sliced
1 hot cherry pepper, sliced

❖ Remove the heavy tough stems of the rabe; rinse in cold water. In a frying pan, sauté garlic in olive oil over medium heat for 5 minutes. Remove the pan from stove; let oil cool for 5 minutes. Add hot pepper and rabe. Return pan to low heat; cover tightly. Steam the rabe for 15 to 20 minutes. Serve hot or cold.

❖ Note: Rabe is good with any meat and is great with a sandwich.

Irish Potato Stuffing

Recipe may be multiplied for up to 30 pounds of potatoes. Believe it or not, this was an Irish grandmother's recipe—Margaret Conlon. The family now serves this instead of potato at holidays, so that's why you may need 30 pounds of potatoes for a real feast.

5 pounds potatoes, peeled and diced
Margarine
Milk
Salt and pepper
1 cup finely chopped onion
1 teaspoon minced garlic
2 ribs celery diced
2 to 3 ounces sweet sausage, chopped in small pieces
3 large eggs
8 ounces dry coarse bread crumbs
1 to 3 tablespoons poultry seasoning

❖ Cook potatoes and prepare as for mashed potatoes with margarine, milk, salt and pepper. In a large skillet, melt 4 tablespoons margarine and sauté onion. Add garlic, celery and sausage, continue to cook about 5 minutes when sausage is cooked. Stir into mashed potatoes. Add eggs and coarse bread crumbs to potatoes, mix well. Use more milk as needed if mixture becomes too thick. Season to taste with salt, pepper and poultry seasoning. Stuff poultry to serve as a side dish.

Walter's "Famous Irish Coffee"

Best at the end of the meal

1 large pot black coffee
1/2 pint heavy cream, whipped
4 tablespoons sugar
Irish Mist

❖ In glass mugs or Irish coffee glasses, put a silver spoon and pour hot coffee, leaving room to pour 2 ounces Irish coffee on top. Put a dollop of heavy cream which has been sweetened with sugar on top of mixture. Do not stir. Serve with straws.

Homemade Manicotti

Sharing disciplines in teaching I feel is an important aspect of education, particularly at the high school level. One teacher who I enjoyed working with was Eleanor Caito Thompson of Scituate High School. Her expertise as a teacher and experience as a "great cook" helped to make my Senior Consumer education classes a little different, especially with Homemade Manicotti.

Elinor says, "Being of Neapolitan Italian heritage, I make the manicotti in this recipe in the southern Italian tradition. The béchamel sauce is a typical northern Italian addition, born of my culinary experience when living in the Veneto region of northern Italy. Like most artists, I love to cook and adjust my recipes according to what I have on hand. Presentation, however, is the key to elegant dining. Place one or two manicotti on an 8-inch dessert plate and serve as a separate course

Elinor's Stuffed Manicotti

Being creative is what Ellie does best and here's an idea for you all. Getting together at family reunions, her cousins "lamented because they had no family history compiled." You guessed it, she put together the family history of both the John B. Caito family and the Gaetano Lancellotti's with the help of some of the family. It included interesting family lore, pictures, recipes and much about customs and habits at mealtime. Something that many of you should consider—a lasting remembrance for all.

Pasta:
3 cups flour

1 tablespoon salt

4 eggs

1 tablespoon oil (about 1/4 cup water if dough is too dry)

prior to the main entrée. Pass a little extra Parmesan cheese on the side."

❖ Mix all ingredients in electric mixer, about 2 minutes until well blended and a stiff dough is formed. You will need a heavy duty mixer to be able to handle this mixture. Knead for 3 minutes. Divide and shape into small patties. Set aside and cover with a cloth; let rest while preparing filling.

Ricotta Filling:
1 pound ricotta cheese

2 eggs

Salt and pepper

1/2 pound mozzarella cheese, shredded

1/2 cup grated Parmesan cheese

❖ Mix together until well blended. Set aside.

Béchamel Sauce:
2 tablespoons butter

3 tablespoons flour

Salt and pepper

Nutmeg

2 cups boiling milk

❖ Melt butter, stir in flour, a little salt, pepper and nutmeg. Add 2 cups boiling milk slowly; stir continuously with wire whisk about 5 minutes. Set aside.

Tomato Gravy (Sauce):

Believe it or not they call it gravy in Rhode Island. My father always called it, "the lifeblood of Italy."

1½ ground beef or sausage taken out of the casing

2 12-ounce cans tomato purée

1 cup water

1 6-ounce can tomato paste

Pinch Italian seasoning

Garlic powder

❖ Sauté meat in microwave and break up. Add tomato purée, water, tomato paste, Italian seasoning and garlic powder to taste. Cook on High for 40 minutes.

Shells:

❖ Use macaroni machine to roll out strips 16 inches long. Layout on clean towels on a table. Cut into 4 sections; if cooking at a later time, allow dough to dry and place on a tray separated by paper towels and sprinkled with cornmeal. Place pasta in a colander, put in boiling water, which has 1 tablespoon oil and salt added to it for about 3 minutes. Do not overcook. Pull up colander and place under cold running water to cool; spread cooked cooked pasta on towels.

Assemble Manicotti:

❖ Place about 2 tablespoons filling on cooked dough. Fold in sides and roll up as shown. Place manicotti with folded sides down in a shallow baking dish that has a thin layer of tomato sauce spread on bottom. Top with layer of Béchamel Sauce, then finally a layer of tomato sauce and Parmesan cheese. Cover with foil. May be frozen now or baked at 425° F for 20 minutes or until bubbly. Uncover last 5 minutes of cooking.

Chicken Pesto

Victor and Dawn Brush, are owner-operators of the Village Deli which is New York-Italian in style. Don't let the name fool you, they're both Italian. The Village Deli features authentic Italian family-style meals to go. Especially good is their Pea and Cheddar cheese soups which are popular with local business people as is their gourmet coffee.

2 cups fresh basil

2/3 cup fresh parsley

1/2 cup pine nuts or walnuts

10 cloves fresh garlic

Olive oil

1 pound linguine

4 whole boneless chicken breasts, about 1 pound

4 fresh tomatoes

1/2 can (8 ounces) black pitted olives

❖ Blend basil, parsley, nuts and garlic together in a food processor. Add enough olive oil to make mixture a thick sauce. Cook linguine according to package directions. Cut chicken into halves; sauté in a little oil until partially cooked. Add fresh tomatoes and pesto; simmer for about 5 to 8 minutes more or until chicken is cooked. Cut olives into small pieces and add to chicken mixture. When linguine is cooked *al dente*, drain and put onto heated platter. Top with chicken and pesto mixture. Serve with Village Deli hard, crusty bread "the Best in Rhode Island" says the *Rhode Island Monthly*. Serves 8.

Jewish Potato Pancakes (Latkes)

A popular American Jewish dish served at family meals as well as during holidays.

1 medium onion, grated
5 or 6 peeled and grated Idaho potatoes
1½ tablespoons matzo meal or flour
¼ teaspoon baking powder
2 eggs, beaten
½ teaspoon salt

❖ Mix all ingredients together. Drop by large spoonfuls onto a greased hot griddle. Fry on both sides until well browned. Serve hot with sour cream or applesauce. If you want them crisp, flatten each well with back of spoon. Turn only once.

❖ Note: Grate onion first, then potato. Mix immediately or the potatoes will turn brown.

Tong Il Kim

This recipe was demonstrated by Tong Il Kim in my International Foods class one day, and I don't know who learned more...Tong, the students or myself, but it was a wonderful cultural exchange...and what a way to teach, certainly beats those worksheets for student involvement, motivation and learning. Paula Sullivan, Tong's ESL teacher assisted him in translating from Korean to English. I might note that this is an excellent program, and it really works in providing services to those who intend to learn English.

Korean Shish Kabob (Sanjog)

4 pieces oriental dried mushrooms
Corn oil
Soy sauce to taste
Sesame oil
Sugar
1 pound lean tender beef
3 pieces Korean rice cake
1 carrot
1 bunch scallions
Sesame seeds

❖ Soak mushrooms in water for awhile, add a little corn oil. In a large bowl mix soy sauce, sesame oil and sugar. Cut beef into ¼-inch by 3-inch pieces. Cut rice cake, peeled carrots, scallions and mushrooms so they can be arranged on bamboo skewers.

❖ Arrange all items, alternating beef, rice cake, mushrooms, etc. Put rice cake in between the other items; beef on the ends. Cover with soy sauce marinade for at least 10 minutes.

❖ Cook the shish kabob in a very large frying pan with a small amount of corn oil until meat is cooked, turning several times. When cooked, place on platter and sprinkle with sesame seed.

❖ Note: Korean rice cake can be purchased at most oriental food stores.

The Brigido's

"In 1919 Maria Josus Elias came to Rhode Island from Lisbon, Portugal, with her mother and sister. They ran a boarding house. In 1920, Augusto G. Brigado came over from Lisbon with his brother and uncle." Needless to say, a few years later Maria and Augusto married and lived in Pawtucket and had three children: Lucille and the twins—Georgianna and George. In 1943, they bought a small convenience store in Pawtucket, which the entire family ran.

The entire family is still involved and in 1993, after 50 years it's still a "family business" although it is part of an independent supermarket chain. George and his two sons, Druce and Mark now have two stores, one in Pascoag and in Scituate as well as "The Indulge Bakery." Keeping it a family business makes it different than any other store. Service and friendliness by George Brigado & Sons (Village IGA's) is a welcome tradition in any community. As George told me, our motto is "Pleasing you pleases us!"

Brigido's Portuguese Stuffing

Lee Ann Brigido Smith writes that this is the "family's favorite."

1 pound linguisa
2 pounds ground pork
3 pounds lean ground beef
8 onions, chopped
6 to 7 loaves white Portuguese bread
3 large eggs
1/4 cup parsley
2 lemons
Salt and pepper

❖ Remove linguisa from casing and cook with pork, beef and chopped onions in a very large frying pan (or 2 if need). Do not drain juices. Put in a large roasting pan. In another large bowl, break apart bread in small bite-sized pieces, then add enough water until bread is moist but not soaked. Add to meat; add beaten eggs, parsley and juice from the lemons. Mix well. Add salt and pepper to taste. Mix it very well. Stuff turkey or chicken and put the remainder in a baking pan or freeze. Bake at 350° F for at least 1/2 hour or until brown on top. Serves 24.

Gloria's Portuguese Soup

2 1/2 to 3-pound beef shank bone with meat
1 pound chourico
1/4 salt pork, optional
1 head kale, cleaned, chopped
1 small Chinese cabbage
4 onions, sliced
4 to 5 carrots, sliced
4 to 6 medium potatoes, chopped
Salt and pepper
2 cups cooked elbow macaroni

❖ Place shank bone in 10 to 12-quart pan and cover with water. Cook for 2 to 2 1/2 hours.

❖ Put chourico in after beef has cooked, about 1 1/2 hours. If using salt pork, add at the same time. Finish cooking beef.

❖ About 20 minutes before beef is done add kale, cabbage, onions, carrots and potatoes. Season with salt and pepper to taste. When almost done add precooked macaroni. Serves 8 to 10.

Flippers
(Portuguese Fried Dough)

1 cup scalded milk
1/2 cup sugar
1 teaspoon salt
1/2 cup butter
1 package yeast
1/4 cup lukewarm water
2 eggs, slightly beaten
5 to 6 cups flour
Corn or vegetable oil
Granulated sugar

❖ To scalded milk, add sugar, salt and butter. Sprinkle yeast into lukewarm water; let stand for 5 minutes. Stir until dissolved. Add yeast mixture and eggs to milk.

❖ Gradually add flour, beating with wooden spoon until too stiff to beat. Place on lightly floured board and knead until smooth and elastic. Form into ball. Place dough in lightly greased bowl; turn dough over so that whole surface is coated with grease. Cover and let rise in warm place until doubled.

❖ Lightly grease your palms and fingers. Break off—don't cut—a handful of dough. Stretch with

fingers into oblong shape and fry in hot corn oil until golden brown on all sides. Test one to make sure it's done inside and not still gooey. Drain on paper towel, sprinkle with sugar or serve with syrup or molasses. Serve warm. Yields about 12.

Spanish Apple-Mint Crisp

1 tablespoon margarine
6 large cooking apples, (about 2½ pounds) peeled, cored and sliced as for apple pie
2 teaspoons cinnamon
2 teaspoons mint leaves or 1 teaspoon mint extract
1¼ cups flour
3/4 cup sugar
3/4 teaspoon baking powder
1 egg
1 cup heavy cream, whipped, or 1 cup all-purpose cream, whipped or 1 cup whipped topping, optional

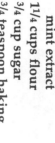

❖ Preheat oven to 350° F.

❖ Put margarine in 2-quart baking dish or 9x9-inch baking pan in oven to melt butter.

❖ Put sliced apples in a bowl and mix lightly with cinnamon and mint. Remove baking dish from oven and put apple mixture in bottom of dish, pressing down lightly.

❖ In a mixing bowl; combine flour, sugar, and baking powder. Add 1 egg and mix with a fork or pastry blender. Sprinkle this mixture over the apples.

❖ Bake for 30 to 40 minutes or until golden brown on top.

❖ Serve warm or cold with whipped cream or topping. Serves 6.

❖ Can be reheated in microwave.

Spanish Fruit Salad

1 16-ounce can chunk pineapple or 1 fresh pineapple
2 navel oranges
1/2 pound seedless grapes
4 apples, Courtland or Delicious
8 leaves green or red leaf lettuce

❖ If using fresh pineapple, peel, remove core and eyes. Slice into 3/4-inch slices and cut into cubes. Peel oranges using a sharp knife to

Spanish Gazpacho

1 medium onion
1/2 green pepper
2 ribs celery
1 clove garlic
1 tablespoon fresh parsley
2 cups tomato juice
1 16-ounce can stewed tomatoes
1/4 cup vinegar
1/4 cup olive oil
White pepper
Tabasco sauce, optional
Croutons

❖ Put first 5 ingredients in blender. Add tomato juice and stewed tomatoes. Add vinegar, oil, white pepper and Tabasco sauce. Chill.

❖ Serve in soup cups. Garnish with croutons.

Spanish Shrimp in Red Rioja Wine

1 medium onion, finely minced
2 cloves garlic, finely minced
3 tablespoons olive oil
1 cup dry red Rioja wine
2 pounds cooked shrimp, shelled
Salt
Cayenne pepper

❖ In a large frying pan, sauté minced onion and garlic in olive oil until transparent.

❖ Add wine all at once and continue simmering until liquid is reduced. Add shrimp and heat through. Add salt and cayenne pepper to taste.

❖ Serve hot or cold. Serves 6 to 8 as an appetizer, 4 to 6 as an entrée.

❖ To cook shrimp: Cover shrimp with water. Bring to a boil, about 5 minutes and shrimp turn pink. Peel and devein shrimp.

---

remove all white membrane from outside of orange. Set aside. Wash grapes and cut in half. Peel and slice apples into thin wedges.

❖ Note: If you are not going to make and serve salad right away, put all fruit in 1 bowl with apples at the bottom. Juice from pineapple and orange will prevent apples from browning. Cover with plastic wrap and refrigerate until ready to use.

❖ To assemble salad: On individual salad plate put 1 leaf lettuce. Top with pineapple, grapes and apples. Slice oranges crosswise and put 2 on each salad. Serve with Honey Orange Dressing.

Honey Orange Dressing

1 cup mayonnaise
1/2 cup honey
1/2 cup orange juice

❖ Use a wire whisk or egg beater to mix all ingredients together well. Serve on side with fruit salad.

Swedish Orange Cookies

1 cup butter, softened
1/2 cup granulated sugar
1/2 cup brown sugar
2 tablespoons grated orange rind
3 tablespoons orange juice
2³/4 cups sifted flour
1 egg white, unbeaten
Broken nuts
Sugar

❖ Cream butter and sugars together. Add orange rind and juice; mix well. Add sifted flour a little at a time until mixture is firm.

❖ Shape into a roll. Chill for at least 1 hour. When ready to bake, slice thin. Brush tops with unbeaten egg white and sprinkle with broken nuts and sugar.

❖ Bake at 350° F until light brown.

❖ Note: Watch carefully as they brown quickly.

Grandma Bloom's Swedish Spritz

1/2 pound butter, softened
2/3 cup sugar
3 egg yolks
1 teaspoon almond flavoring
2¹/2 cups flour

❖ Cream together butter, sugar and egg yolks.

❖ Add almond flavoring and gradually add flour.

❖ Put through cookie press following press directions.

❖ Bake at 400° F for 10 to 12 minutes.

❖ Note: Watch as they brown quickly.

Fresh Fruit with Swiss Chocolate Plunge

2/3 cup light or dark corn syrup
1/2 cup heavy cream
1 8-ounce package semi-sweet Swiss chocolate, chopped

❖ In a medium saucepan, bring corn syrup and cream to a boil.

❖ Remove and add chocolate, continue stirring until melted. Serve with fresh fruit and toothpicks. Make 1 1/2 cups.

Syrian Apricot Candy

2 pounds dried apricots
Blanched almonds
1/2 cup sugar

❖ Steam apricots in colander over water until tender.

❖ Put through food chopper or food processor. Add sugar and form into small patties.

❖ Place a blanched almond on each pattie and roll in sugar. Place in a paper holder.

Dessert the Table

Angel Food Quickie

A favorite for those who want a quick easy no-bake dessert

1 angel food cake
1 3-ounce package fruit gelatin
1/2 cup hot water
1 cup cold water
1 cup fruit, drained (peaches, blueberries, strawberries, etc.)
1 cup heavy cream, whipped or whipped topping
Fruit for garnish

❖ Take one angel food cake and slice cake 1 inch down from the top. Remove and set aside. Make a tunnel completely around the remaining cake, being careful not to break through the sides or bottom. Save cake cubes you have removed. In a bowl dissolve gelatin in hot water. Add cold water, fruit and cake cubes. Put in refrigerator till almost set, about 1 hour. Pour in place that you have scooped out. Put top back on cake, if needed put a couple of toothpicks to secure. Refrigerate at least 6 hours or overnight. Just before serving, frost with whipped cream and garnish with fruit. Serves 6 to 8.

Boiled Custard

This is a basic dessert sauce which can be used for many desserts.

1 cup milk
2 egg yolks
2 tablespoons sugar
1/2 teaspoon vanilla

❖ Using a double boiler, scald milk over hot water. In a bowl beat egg yolks and sugar. Pour milk slowly over egg mixture. Return to double boiler, stirring constantly, about 5 minutes or until custard thickens enough to coat spoon. Cool and add vanilla.

Custard á l'Orange

4 eggs
1/2 cup sugar
1/4 teaspoon salt
3 cups milk, heated until very warm
1 teaspoon vanilla

❖ Beat eggs, sugar and salt together until well blended. Gradually stir in milk. Add vanilla. Pour into six (6-ounce) custard cups. Set in large baking pan. Pour very hot water into pan to within 1/2 inch of top of custard. Bake in preheated 350° F oven 25 to 30 minutes or until knife inserted near center comes out clean. Promptly remove from hot water. Chill thoroughly, at least 3 hours. To remove custard from cups: gently loosen at top with narrow spatula or knife and invert onto serving plate. Spoon about 2 tablespoons Orange Sauce over each custard.

Orange Sauce

1/4 cup sugar
1 tablespoon cornstarch
2/3 cup orange juice
1 tablespoon lemon juice
1/2 to 1 teaspoon grated orange rind

❖ In small saucepan combine 1/4 cup sugar and 1 tablespoon cornstarch. Gradually pour 2/3 cup orange juice and 1 tablespoon lemon juice into sugar mixture, stirring until blended. Cook and stir until mixture boils and is smooth and thickened. Boil for 1 minute, stirring constantly. Remove from heat. Stir in grated orange peel, if desired. Cool slightly before serving. Makes about 3/4 cup.

Grapes with Crème Fraîche

Although this is not a true Martha's Vineyard recipe, it has "the Vineyard flavor" of the grapes that gave it its name. Very simple and refreshing.

2 cups red grapes, halved, seeded
2 cups green grapes, halved, seeded
2 cups blue/black grapes, halved and seeded
1/4 cup orange liqueur or orange juice
1/8 teaspoon ground cinnamon
Crème Fraîche

❖ Combine grapes, liqueur and cinnamon; stir to coat grapes. Cover; refrigerate several hours. Spoon into serving dish; top with Crème Fraîche. Makes 8 servings.

Crème Fraîche

1 cup heavy cream
1 tablespoon buttermilk

❖ Combine cream and buttermilk; mix thoroughly. Cover; let stand at room temperature overnight or until lightly thickened. Refrigerate 24 hours before serving. Makes 1 cup.

Lemon Pecan Pie

A nice change from traditional pecan pie—not as rich. Would also make an excellent filling for miniature tarts.

3 eggs
1/3 cup margarine, melted
1 1/2 cups granulated sugar
3/4 cup pecans or walnuts
1 teaspoon lemon extract
2 tablespoons lemon juice
1 8 or 9-inch unbaked pie shell

❖ Beat eggs well, but not foamy. Add all other ingredients and pour into pie shell. Bake for 50 to 60 minutes in a 300° F oven. Top with whipped cream or serve plain. Serves 6 to 8.

Sweetie Pie's Best Ice Cream

1 quart light cream
1 1/2 cups sugar
2 tablespoons pure vanilla
1 pint heavy cream

❖ In a saucepan, heat and stir light cream and sugar over medium heat until sugar is completely dissolved. Cool completely. Stir in vanilla and heavy cream. Chill 1 to 2 hours. Freeze in crank-type freezer, as on page 142.

Coffee Ice Cream

❖ Use basic recipe for vanilla ice cream, but add 1/3 cup instant coffee to light cream and sugar. Follow remainder of basic vanilla ice cream recipe.

Chocolate Ice Cream

❖ Use basic recipe for vanilla ice cream, but add 3 ounces unsweetened chocolate to light cream and increase sugar to 2 cups. Follow remainder of basic recipe.

Smithfield Historical Society Ice Cream Social

The Smithfield Historical Society's Ice Cream Social is a successful fundraiser and a real summer funfest. Members in colonial costume serve up gallons of homemade ice cream and a variety of homemade toppings.

Smith-Appleby House Famous Vanilla Ice Cream

You may have youngsters on hand to lick the paddle, one of the joys of childhood which is not readily available today.

1½ cups sugar
¼ cup flour
½ teaspoon salt
1 quart milk
4 eggs, beaten
4 cups whipping cream
3 tablespoons vanilla
Rock salt
S & S Farm Toppings (see page 78)

❖ In a 3-quart saucepan, thoroughly mix the sugar, flour and salt. Gradually add milk and stir until ingredients are thoroughly combined and mixture is smooth. Cook the mixture over medium high heat, stirring constantly with wooden spoon, until slightly thickened and bubbly. Remove from heat. Stir about 1 cup of the hot mixture into the beaten eggs very gradually, then add the egg mixture to the remaining hot mixture in the saucepan.

❖ Cook over medium heat, stirring constantly, for 1 minute. Chill this mixture. When thoroughly chilled, stir in the whipping cream and vanilla. Pour the chilled mixture into a freezer can up to 2/3 capacity. (If using an electric freezer, follow the manufacturer's directions.) Fit can securely into ice cream freezer. Adjust dasher; cover with lid.

❖ Pack alternate layers of crushed ice and rock salt into the outer container. Use 6 parts ice to 1 part salt. Turn handle slowly at first and continue turning until it becomes difficult to turn handle. Remove ice to below the level of the can lid so that no melted ice seeps into the can.

❖ Wipe can and lid with a damp cloth to remove salt and ice. Remove lid and dasher, scraping ice cream from the dasher back into the can.

❖ Cover the can with several layers of waxed paper or foil. Plug the opening in the lid with a cork. Replace lid. Pack additional ice and salt into the outer container. Use 4 parts ice to 1 part salt. Cover freezer with heavy cloth. Let ripen about 4 hours. Serve with toppings.

Recipe from "Recipes from the Smith-Appleby House" by Historical Society of Smithfield, Rhode Island

Raspberry Sherbet

This was found in many old cookbooks of the area and was introduced about 1902 by Knox Gelatine and appeared to be very popular, as well as refreshing.

1 pint raspberries
2¼ cups sugar
Juice of 2 lemons
1 tablespoon gelatin (dissolved in cold water)
1 quart boiling water

❖ Mash raspberries and add a little water. Bring to a boil and strain. In another bowl, mix sugar and juice of 2 lemons, let stand. Mix gelatin in 1/4 cup cold water. Add 1 quart boiling water. Cool, then add to lemon and raspberry juices. Pour in refrigerator trays and freeze. Just before serving give the frozen dessert a twirl in your food processor or blender...be careful not to make a drink out of it. Top with a sprig of mint and you're all set.

Anne's Pavlova

The Pearsons were this served at an Australian Barbie (cookout) on a recent trip to Australia and New Zealand. Their friend, Anne, used canned fruit to decorate her Pavlova. Pavlova was originated in Perth, Western Australia, in the early 1900s when Pavlova, a famous Russian ballerina, traveled widely with her own company and visited Perth. She performed with a lightness and grace that few ballet dancers have ever achieved, so the story goes. This dessert was so light that it was named Pavlova.

1 cup egg whites, at room temperature
2 rounded teaspoons cornstarch
1 teaspoon white vinegar
1½ cups sugar
½ teaspoon vanilla
3 tablespoons boiling water
1½ cups whipping cream
1 tablespoon sugar
1 teaspoon vanilla
1½ teaspoons plain gelatin
1½ tablespoons boiling water
Fruit for top—bananas and strawberries or kiwi pineapple, oranges/pineapple (fresh or canned)

❖ Put egg whites in a deep bowl, being sure no yolk gets in white.

❖ Add cornstarch and white vinegar and start to beat.

❖ Gradually add 1½ cups sugar 2 tablespoons at a time until all is used. Slowly beat in vanilla and boiling water until stiff and glossy, but not dry. It will take from 10 to 15 minutes to beat, depending on the type of mixer you are using...be careful not to overbeat.

❖ Draw a 10½-inch circle on brown or parchment paper and place on a cookie sheet.

❖ Heap mixture on circle and spread evenly as possible with a slight dip in the middle.

❖ Place sheet in the middle of a 350° F oven for 10 minutes then lower temperature to 200° F for 1½ hours. Turn off oven and leave it until cold. (Overnight is a good idea.)

❖ Using a spatula, carefully slide Pavlova onto a 12 to 13-inch serving dish depending on how much it has spread.

❖ The middle will sink a bit. (Sometimes it cracks, usually when you want it for special events.) The inside of the Pavlova will be the consistency of marshmallow.

❖ To complete dessert: Whip 1½ cups cream with 1 tablespoon sugar and vanilla until stiff. (If this is to stand a while before serving, add the following: gelatin which has been dissolved in boiling water. Cool. Add to whipped cream.) Spread whipped cream on Pavlova shell and decorate with fruit. Serves 8 to 12 easily.

Hazel's Suet Pudding

1 cup ground suet
1 cup molasses
1 cup milk
1 pound raisins
1 teaspoon cinnamon
1/2 teaspoon each cloves and allspice
1 teaspoon salt
1 teaspoon baking soda
About 5 cups flour

❖ Beat all ingredients together well, adding enough flour to make a stiff batter. Grease pans well. Steam 3 hours. If you do not have a real steamer, use two 1-pound coffee cans covered tightly with foil and secured with string. Put on a rack in a deep pan. Add water about half way up can. Cover and steam. Serve with Hard Sauce or Cooked "Soft Sauce."

Hard Sauce

1 stick butter
1 pound confectioners' sugar
1 teaspoon vanilla
Milk

❖ Mix softened butter with sifted confectioners' sugar and vanilla. If very difficult to handle add a little milk.

Rumford Hard Sauce

Enough for one dessert of almost any kind. Tastes best when spooned over hot dessert, since it melts immediately.

1/3 cup margarine, softened
1 cup confectioners' sugar
2 tablespoons boiling water
1/2 teaspoon vanilla
1/4 teaspoon ground nutmeg

❖ Using a hand mixer, cream margarine as for cake, gradually add sugar and water. When very light and fluffy, add vanilla and nutmeg. Chill.

❖ Note: The addition of water makes the sauce lighter and lessens the labor of beating. May be stored in a covered container in refrigerator for weeks.

Cooked "Soft Sauce"

2 tablespoons cornstarch
2 cups water
2 tablespoons butter
Dash of salt
1/2 teaspoon nutmeg

❖ Mix cornstarch in a little water and add to 2 cups water. Cook in double boiler, stirring often till thickened. Add butter, salt and nutmeg. Serve hot.

Anna Clearwater's Indian Bread Pudding

1 loaf day old bread
2 eggs
1 cup milk
1/2 cup sugar
1 teaspoon vanilla
1/2 teaspoon cinnamon
Pinch of salt
1 cup raisins
1 tablespoon butter

❖ Soak bread in water until soft; squeeze water out. Beat eggs and add milk, sugar, vanilla, cinnamon and salt. Mix in with soaked bread;

Indian Pudding

add raisins and stir together. Melt butter and add to mixture. Grease 1½ to 2-quart baking dish with butter. Spoon batter into baking dish. Bake at 300° F for 1 hour or until light brown.

Indian Pudding

3 cups milk
6 tablespoons cornmeal
¼ teaspoon salt
1 tablespoon butter
¾ teaspoon cinnamon
¼ teaspoon ginger
¾ cup dark Karo
1 egg, beaten
½ cup cold milk

❖ Scald 3 cups of milk in double boiler, stir in meal slowly until smooth. Cook for 15 minutes.

❖ Add remaining ingredients except the ½ cup cold milk. Turn into buttered casserole and carefully pour the ½ cup cold milk over pudding so it will stay on top. Place dish in pan of water. Bake for 3 hours at 300° F. Serve hot with cream, softened ice cream or vanilla sauce.

Orange Pudding

4 oranges
½ cup sugar
1 quart milk
4 eggs, separated
1 cup sugar
4 tablespoons cornstarch
4 tablespoons sugar

❖ Peel and slice oranges and place in the bottom of a 1½-quart baking dish. Sprinkle ½ cup sugar over oranges.

❖ Scald the milk and beat in 4 egg yolks, 1 cup of sugar and cornstarch. Continue stirring until mixture is thickened. Pour over oranges while hot, mixing thoroughly.

❖ Beat 4 egg whites until stiff, adding 4 tablespoons of sugar gradually. Spoon on top of orange pudding mixture.

❖ Bake in a 425° F oven until meringue is lightly browned. Cool.

Coffee Jelly

A tasty light dessert

2 cups strong black coffee
1 envelope unflavored gelatin
¼ cup sugar or
2 to 3 packages sugar substitute

❖ Sprinkle 1 envelope of gelatin over ½ cup of cold coffee; stir well and let stand for 1 minute.

❖ Add 1½ cups of boiling coffee to gelatin mixture, adding sugar. Stir until all is dissolved.

❖ Put in individual dessert dishes or in 2 to 3-cup bowl. Cool; refrigerate until firm.

❖ Variation: ½ cup cold coffee mixed with gelatin, then add 1 cup hot coffee and sugar. Stir well. Put in refrigerator, chill until consistency of unbeaten egg white. Beat in ½ cup evaporated milk. Chill in refrigerator until firm.

❖ Note: Both may be served plain, with a little milk or whipped cream or topping.

Black Chocolate Cake

1½ cups flour
1 cup sugar
1/4 teaspoon salt
2 ounces unsweetened chocolate
1 tablespoon margarine
1 teaspoon baking soda
1 cup sweet milk
1 egg
1 teaspoon vanilla

❖ Sift flour, sugar and salt together. Melt 2 squares of chocolate with margarine. Dissolve baking soda in 1 cup milk.

❖ Add all ingredients together and beat well. Pour into 2 greased 8-inch cake pans.

❖ Bake at 350° F for 25 to 30 minutes.

❖ Use your favorite frosting.

Funny Cake

Judged at Foster Center Old Home Days in 4-H baking division

2 eggs, beaten
1 cup brown sugar, packed
5 tablespoons flour
1/8 teaspoon baking soda
Pinch of salt
3/4 cup chopped walnuts
3 tablespoons margarine, melted

❖ Preheat oven to 350° F.

❖ Combine eggs and brown sugar, beat until well blended. Add flour, baking soda, salt, walnuts and melted margarine.

❖ Spread mixture in a well-buttered 8-inch round cake pan.

❖ Bake for 20 minutes. Cool for 5 minutes. Turn upside down, sprinkle with confectioners' sugar.

❖ This simple cake keeps well, if it doesn't disappear in a flash.

Sour Milk Raisin Cake

1 cup sugar
1/3 cup shortening
2 eggs
1/2 cup sour milk
3/4 cup raisins, chopped
1¼ teaspoons baking soda
2 cups flour
Raspberry preserves
Confectioners' sugar

❖ Cream together sugar and shortening, then add eggs, beat until fluffy. Stir in sour milk and raisins. Add baking soda and flour which has been sifted together. When well beaten, pour into two 8-inch greased cake pans.

❖ Bake at 350° F for 25 to 30 minutes or until cake starts to pull away from the edge.

❖ Spread 1 layer with raspberry preserves, put second layer on top and dust with confectioners' sugar.

Peggy's Annual Cookie Exchange

On Jamestown Island, an event has taken place for a number of years that many of you might like to try. Peggy Burse, a free-lance home economist, and her friends join together on the 15th of December for their "Cookie Exchange." Peg tells me for it to run smoothly some basic rules must be followed. Briefly I will try to outline them for your use.

1. Bring 4 dozen homemade cookies of the same kind. Rule of thumb—double your recipe and bring all of them. For large cookies, such as gingerbread men Christmas trees or Santa faces, bring one for each person attending, plus a few extra if one happens to break.

2. Those attending should bring their favorite recipe, unless you have been attending from the beginning. Those that are all-timers at this should bring a new recipe each time.

3. Put cookies in container with your name, number of cookies, recipe for cookies in container taped on and an empty container with your name for your take home goodies.

4. Copies of your recipe with helpful suggestions and your name for the number of persons attending.

5. Attire: Colors are red and green for the season—remember it's a festive occasion.

6. *If you want to participate and can't come on the 15th, follow all the rules and bring your cookies to Peggy beforehand.*

7. *Peggy divides the number of cookies by the number of people attending. She says 26 is her limit. All cookies not included in exchange are donated to a deserving family or persons on Jamestown who otherwise would not have cookies of the season; in addition, each person brings a staple food item for a gift basket for someone on the island. Sounds like a good idea to me.*

Peggy features a Dessert and Beverage Buffet for all those attending. Examples of her talents include Apple Flambé Cake, Chocolate Zebra Cheesecake, Fruit with Plunge and a Giant Cranberry Turnover. Beverages include all nonalcoholic specialties: Apple Wassail, Holiday Raspberry Punch, Irish Cream Decaffeinated Coffee and assorted teas.

Apricot Nut Snowball

No-bake and oh, so easy.

6 ounces dried apricots
¼ cup apricot jam
1 tablespoon sugar
1 cup chopped nuts
1 cup sweetened coconut

❖ Put all ingredients in food processor and pulse until a mass is formed.

❖ Form balls using a rounded tea-spoon and roll in confectioners' sugar.

❖ Chill, covered loosely, in refrigerator.

❖ Note: Wet hands with water when rounding cookies.

Nancy's Cardamom Cookies

1 cup butter (2 sticks)
2 teaspoons baking soda
1 teaspoon ground cardamom
1/2 teaspoon salt
2 cups brown sugar, packed
2 eggs
4 1/2 cups flour
2 teaspoons cream of tartar

❖ Cream together softened butter, baking soda, cardamom and salt. Blend in brown sugar. Beat in eggs.

❖ Sift together flour and cream of tartar, gradually stir into batter.

❖ Chill dough for 3 to 4 hours.

❖ Preheat oven to 350° F.

❖ Make 1/2-inch balls and place on ungreased cookie sheet, press top with fork. Cookie press may also be used.

❖ Bake for 10 minutes. Cool and store in tightly covered container. Makes 8 dozen.

Jane's No-Bake Congo Bars

Jane vows she will not bake for an Art Festival meeting, but she'll make these bars, which we all think she can make in her sleep...P.S. You do have to bake them in a preheated 350° F oven.

1 pound package brown sugar
3 eggs
1/2 cup vegetable oil
1 cup chocolate chips
1 cup nuts, chopped
2 teaspoons vanilla
2 1/2 cups flour
2 1/2 teaspoons baking powder
1/4 teaspoon salt

❖ Beat together brown sugar, eggs and vegetable oil. Mix in chocolate chips, nuts, and vanilla. Add flour, baking powder and salt. Continue beating until mixture is well mixed.

❖ Spread in 9x16-inch jelly roll pan.

❖ Bake at 350° F for 30 to 35 minutes. Let cool before removing from pan.

Jill's Oatmeal Crunchies

1 cup flour
1/2 cup sugar
1/2 teaspoon baking powder
1/4 teaspoon baking soda
1/4 teaspoon salt
1/2 cup brown sugar
1 egg
1/2 teaspoon vanilla
3/4 cup oats

❖ Sift together flour, sugar, baking powder, baking soda and salt in large bowl.

❖ In another bowl, cream together brown sugar and shortening and then beat in egg until mixture is soft. Add to the dry ingredients, then add vanilla and oats. Mix.

❖ Shape by tablespoonfuls into small balls. Dip tops into sugar. Place on ungreased cookie sheet.

❖ Bake at 350° F for 12 to 15 minutes.

Carl's Oatmeal Raisin Cookies

1/4 cup margarine
3/4 cup sugar
1/4 cup molasses
1 teaspoon vanilla
1 egg or 1/4 cup egg substitute
1 cup flour
1 cup uncooked regular oats or
   1 1/4 cups quick-cooking oats
1/2 teaspoon baking soda
1/2 teaspoon salt
1 teaspoon ground cinnamon
1/2 teaspoon ground ginger
1/2 cup raisins

❖ Cream margarine, gradually add sugar, beating until well blended. Add molasses, vanilla and egg; beat well. Combine flour, oats, baking soda, salt, cinnamon and ginger. Gradually add to creamed mixture, beating well. Add raisins. Drop dough by scant tablespoonfuls 2 inches apart on cookie sheet coated with cooking spray. Bake at 350° F for 8 minutes. Cool for 3 minutes. Remove from pans, cool on wire racks. Makes 3 dozen 2-inch cookies.

Orange Cookies

1/2 cup butter or margarine
1 cup brown sugar
1 egg
1 1/2 cups flour
1 teaspoon baking powder
1/2 teaspoon ginger
1/2 teaspoon baking soda
Grated rind of 1 orange
1 cup chopped nuts

❖ Cream butter and sugar thoroughly. Add egg and mix well.

❖ Add dry ingredients, grated orange rind, and nuts. Make into small balls about the size of walnuts.

❖ Press into shape by dipping a water glass in granulated sugar and pressing down until desired thickness.

❖ Bake at 375° F for 12 to 15 minutes.

4-H Fair Winner Peanut Butter Cookies

Dough may be rolled and cut as desired or a cookie roll can be made, wrapped and refrigerated or frozen for slicing and baking later—just like that found in your dairy case but with your favorite recipe!

1 cup shortening
1 cup sugar
1 cup brown sugar
1 teaspoon vanilla
2 eggs, beaten
1 cup peanut butter, any type
3 cups flour
2 teaspoons baking soda
Dash of salt

❖ Cream shortening, sugars and vanilla. Add eggs; beat well, then stir in peanut butter. Sift together flour, baking powder and salt, stir into creamed mixture. Form into tiny balls, about the size of a walnut, place on an ungreased cookie sheet. Flatten with the bottom of a juice glass or crisscross using the lines of a fork. Bake at 375° F for about 10 minutes. Remove and put on a cooling rack. Makes about 8 dozen.

Portuguese Cookies

2 egg yolks
1 pound margarine
1 pound ricotta cheese
4 cups flour
1 16-ounce (about 4 cups) bag chopped nuts
1¼ cups sugar
1 tablespoon cinnamon
¼ cup milk

❖ Beat egg yolks, margarine and cheese together, stir in flour until well mixed. Refrigerate overnight.

❖ Mix nuts, sugar, cinnamon and milk together for filling.

❖ Remove dough from refrigerator and divide into 5 equal pieces, roll out to 1/4 inch thick 8x12-inch rectangle.

❖ Put 1 cup filling on dough and roll like a log. Make 1/2 to 3/4-inch slices.

❖ Place on ungreased cookie sheet; bake at 400° F for 30 to 35 minutes. Cool.

Specialty-of-the-House Cookies

3 eggs
3/4 cup sugar
1 cup flour
1 teaspoon baking powder
1/8 teaspoon salt
1 teaspoon vanilla
1 cup heavy cream, whipped
Maraschino cherries

❖ Beat eggs until thick. Add sugar and continue beating, gradually adding sifted dry ingredients. Add vanilla.

❖ Drop by tablespoonfuls onto a greased cookie sheet.

❖ Bake at 400° F for about 5 minutes or until done.

❖ Remove from cookie sheet, quickly pinch together 1 side to make a pocket.

❖ When cool, fill with whipped cream, top with 1/2 a cherry.

The Pascoag Gastronomic Society

Twice each year, or more, some of Rhode Island's best known lawmakers, lawyers, doctors, business leaders, religious and political leaders have gathered quietly by the shores of Lake Pascoag for an unparalleled evening of dining and camaraderie. This group has met together for over 30 years with their founder, Fernand E. LaMontagne, a dentist in Pawtucket, who has become known as "the chief." "We select and butcher our own meats, and we spend a lot of time researching our entrées and wines. We plan the menu very carefully and take very special pride in our presentation and preparation," says the Chief. Such delicacies as Cream of Chicken Soup with Egg and Lemon Sauce, Coquilles Saint Jacques, Shrimp Scampi and the favorite which I included in this book, his wife Bernice's Kiss Pie. This group is not a closed *group, and you may be lucky enough to know a member who is allowed to bring one or two guests and receive "an invite" to one of the "top tables" in the Islands. See you there.*

Bernice's Kiss Pie

6 egg whites
1/2 teaspoon cream of tartar
1 teaspoon vanilla
1/2 cup plus 1 tablespoon sugar
1 cup confectioners' sugar, sifted
2 cups heavy cream, whipped
1 1/2 cups peanut brittle, crushed

❖ Line 2 cookie sheets with brown paper. Mark a 10-inch circle on each paper. Preheat oven to 250° F. Beat egg whites until frothy, add cream of tartar and vanilla and beat until very soft peaks form when beater is raised. Gradually beat in sugar 2 tablespoons at a time, beating until very stiff peaks form. Fold in confectioners' sugar. Spread over each circle on paper.

❖ Bake at 250° F for 1 hour. Turn heat off; leave in oven for 2 hours or to overnight with door closed. Place 1 layer on serving plate, spread with

half the whipped cream, sprinkle with half the peanut brittle. Top with second shell, whipped cream and peanut brittle. Chill.

Pecan Brownie Pie

4 eggs
1 3/4 cups sugar
1/4 teaspoon salt
1 cup chopped pecans
2 1/2 squares unsweetened chocolate, melted with
3 tablespoons margarine
1 9-inch unbaked pie shell

❖ Cream together eggs and sugar. Add remaining ingredients and mix well. Pour into unbaked pie shell. Pie pan must measure 9 inches inside of pan.

❖ Bake at 375° F for 25 to 30 minutes or until brown. Cool. (Filling will set while cooling.)

❖ Top with whipped cream or ice cream. Serves 6 to 8.

❖ Note: Use frozen pie shell for quick and easy!

Rhubarb Meringue Pie

3 cups diced rhubarb
2 tablespoons flour
1 1/2 cups sugar
1/8 teaspoon salt
3 egg yolks
1 8-inch unbaked pie shell
3 egg whites
3 tablespoons confectioners' sugar

❖ Wash, dice and flour pieces of rhubarb. Add mixture of beaten sugar, salt and egg yolks.

❖ Mix; turn into unbaked pie shell and bake at 450° F for 10 minutes.

❖ Bake at 325° F for 20 minutes longer. Beat egg whites until stiff, gradually adding confectioners' sugar.

❖ Spread meringue roughly on pie and return to 325° F oven for about 30 minutes more.

Anniversary Pie

Our anniversary is in June and so are strawberries and raspberries, so it's Anniversary Pie!

- 1 9-inch baked pie shell
- 3 pints fresh strawberries
- 1 pint raspberries
- 1/2 cup granulated sugar
- 3 tablespoons cornstarch
- 1/2 pint heavy cream, whipped and sweetened

❖ Bake pie shell. Cool completely. Select best pint of strawberries and set aside for top. Fill bottom of pie shell with 3/4 remaining whole strawberries. Put remaining berries in a 2-quart saucepan with raspberries, 1/2 cup sugar and 1/2 cup water. Bring to a boil and mash berries. Strain only if seeds are not wanted or a clear glace is desired. Reheat strawberry-raspberry mixture to a boil; stir in cornstarch which has been dissolved in about 2 tablespoons of cold water. Continue boiling and stir constantly until thickened. Partially cool. Add last pint of hulled berries to filled pie shell putting stem side down. Tip of strawberry should be pointed up. Pour glace over entire pie, being careful not to get it on edge of crust. Glace should run down between berries. Chill at least 2 hours. Top with whipped heavy cream and serve immediately.

❖ Note: Should be made the same day it is to be served.

Rice Pie

For those who shouldn't

- 1/2 cup egg substitute or 2 eggs
- 1 teaspoon oil
- 1 cup low-fat milk
- 1½ packets sugar substitute
- 1 teaspoon vanilla
- 3/4 cup crushed pineapple
- 4 tablespoons pineapple juice
- 2/3 cup low-fat ricotta cheese
- 1 cup cooked rice
- 1 9-inch pie shell, uncooked

❖ Beat eggs with oil, beating well. Add other ingredients and mix well. Pour into pie shell. Sprinkle with cinnamon and nutmeg. Bake at 350° F for 30 to 40 minutes.

Pie Shell

- 2 tablespoons oil
- 1 cup flour
- 2½ to 3½ tablespoons cold low-fat milk

❖ With a pastry blender, gradually add 1 tablespoon of oil to flour until pieces are the size of peas.

❖ Add milk a little at a time, tossing dough lightly after each addition until dough forms a ball.

❖ Place on a lightly floured surface and roll 1/8 inch thick.

❖ Fit into a 9-inch pie pan.

References

Many of you may be interested in doing more reading about "the Islands." Included are some of the more pertinent sources which I used. Individual cookbook references, receipt books and diaries are too numerous to mention. If the reader is interested in more information, contact the publisher.

Bearse, Roy, ed. Massachusetts: *A Guide to the Pilgrim State.* Boston: Houghton, 1971.

Brown, Richard D. *Massachusetts: A Bicentennial History.* New York: Norton, 1978.

Burroughs, Polly. *Exploring Martha's Vineyard.* Riverside: The Chatham Press, 1973.

Conley, Patrick T. *An Album of Rhode Island History, 1636–1986.* Norfolk: Donning, 1986.

Haley, John Williams. *Old Stone Bank History of Rhode Island. Vol. 1–4.*

Lippincott, Betram. *Indians, Privateers and High Society: A Rhode Island Sampler.* New York: J.B. Lippincott Co., 1986.

McLaughlin, William Gerald. *Rhode Island: A Bicentennial History.* New York: W.W. Norton, 1978.

Rhode Island: A Brief History. Rhode Island State Board of Education. Providence: 1952.

Rhode Island, A Bibliography of its History. Prepared by the Committee for a New England Bibliography; edited by Roger Parks. Hanover: University Press of New England, 1983.

St. Livermore. *History of Block Island Rhode Island.* The Block Island Tercentenary Anniversary Committee, 1961.

Woodward, Carl R. *Plantation in Yankeeland.* Chester: Pequot Press, 1971.

Wright, Marion I. and Robert J. Sullivan. *The Rhode Island Atlas.* Providence: Publications Soc., 1982.

Acknowledgements

Marion King Wieselquist ("Sweetie Pie")

Margot, Adrienne and Tammy for all those Fridays and my "office space"

All the staff of North Scituate Public Library and their patience

Kathi Masi and Pauline Muller, part of my past history and my "honest" readers

Going Place's Travel, Scituate, Rhode Island

"The Saturday Coffee Klatsch"—Ellen, Phil, Jane, Sigrid and Benno and any others who may have happened by!

"The Chief" of the Pascoag Gastronomical Society

The Chambers of Commerce of Nantucket, Martha's Vineyard, Newport, Block Island, Providence, South County; Massachusetts and Rhode Island Development Councils; Historical Societies of Rhode Island, Prudence Island, Jamestown, Block Island, Martha's Vineyard and Nantucket.

The Northern Rhode Island Extension Service, Cooperative Extension Service of the University of Rhode Island and the Cooperative Extension office of Dukes County, Massachusetts.

Advice and assistance given by home economists Robin Kline, CHE of the National Pork Producers Council and Linda Compton, CHE of Ocean Spray Cranberry.

All those who tasted and gave their frank opinion. A special thank you to Marion Wright, Evelyn Kaiman, Peg Brackett, Aichu Stetson, Nancy Stetson, Millie Delahunty, CHE, Elinor Thompson, Martha Patnoad, CHE, The DiPippo's, Ruth Cummings, who helped in "our goings" and so many, many others who shared their experiences and recipes.

A special, special thank you to my heritage and those who taught me to appreciate and to continue mealtime as an act of love on the cook's part; my Grandmother, Lillian Williams Sherman, who taught me you had to get up early to win the prize; my father Robert Williams Sherman, who taught me it was important to do it right; and my mother Blanche Eileen Sherman, that "patience was the best virtue and next humility."

And last, but not least, "The Mary's of Favorite Recipes® Press" especially Mary Cummings for "everything" and to Bill Branch, a real professional who convinced us "we could do it!"

Index

Cookbook Order Form

Stetson Laboratories, Inc.

P.O. Box 822

No. Scituate, RI 02857

(401) 647-3616

Photocopies accepted.

Your Order	Qty	Price	Total
The Island Cookbook	____	× $16.95 =	$ _____
Postage and handling	____	× $ 3.95 =	$ _____
R.I. residents add (7% sales tax)	____	× $ 1.20 =	$ _____
		Subtotal	$ _____
It's Rhode Island—A Cookbook	____	× $ 8.95 =	$ _____
Postage and handling	____	× $ 3.50 =	$ _____
R.I. residents add (7% sales tax)	____	× $ .65 =	$ _____
		Subtotal	$ _____
		Total	$ _____

(Make checks payable to Stetson Laboratories, Inc.)

Sold To: (Please print)

Name _____

Address _____

City _____ State _____ Zip _____

Ship To: (If different address)

Name _____

Address _____

City _____ State _____ Zip _____

[   ] I would like a signed copy personalized for _____

For information about
other cookbooks by this author
Call (401) 647-3616